hamlyn

great
greens!

First published in Great Britain in 2003 by
Hamlyn, a division of Octopus Publishing Group Ltd
2–4 Heron Quays, London E14 4JP

ISBN 0 600 60771 2

A CIP catalogue record for this book is available from
the British Library

Printed and bound in China

10 9 8 7 6 5 4 3 2 1

great
greens!

introduction

contents

what's so
great about greens?

Why eat the recommended five portions of fruit and vegetables each day? Because the benefits to your health, whatever your age, are immense. You can boost your immune system. Protect against cancer, stroke and heart disease. Help to keep your blood pressure and weight at healthy levels. In general, vegetables show slightly more health benefits than fruit, and green vegetables have the most benefits of all.

What are 'greens'?

'Greens' incorporate a number of different groups of vegetables. This book focuses on:
- Asparagus, green peppers, peas, green beans and seaweed.
- Leafy vegetables and salad greens (chard, endive, lettuce, rocket, spinach, vine leaves and watercress)
- Brassicas – a sub-group of the large cruciferous family (broccoli, Brussels sprouts, cabbages, spring greens and kale).

Impressive nutritional credentials

The beneficial effects attributed to eating your greens are down to important nutrients and other powerful biochemical compounds known as phytochemicals that green vegetables contain. Besides fibre, which helps our digestive tract, most green vegetables are rich in folic acid, vitamin C, carotenoids (pigments like beta-carotene, lutein and lycopene), vitamin K and calcium, and may also provide small amounts of iron, zinc and other minerals. Of all the green vegetables, broccoli is probably the richest in disease-protective nutrients.

The levels of the nutrients in greens appear to be linked to the presence of chlorophyll, the green pigment in plants produced by photosynthesis. Basically, the darker green the vegetable, the more nutrients it contains.

Antioxidant action

Antioxidants help protect against free radicals, the highly unstable molecules that cause minor infections and serious degenerative diseases like cancer and heart disease, as well as conditions that come with premature ageing. Green vegetables are a great source of powerful antioxidants such as beta-carotene (which turns to vitamin A in the body) and vitamin C. Other antioxidants include selenium, manganese and zinc, and some of the B vitamins.

The goodies in greens

- Antioxidants (e.g. beta-carotene, vitamins C and E, plus certain minerals)
- B vitamins
- Calcium, magnesium and other major minerals
- Carotenoids (e.g. lutein, lycopene, beta-carotene)
- Chlorophyll
- Fibre
- Folic acid
- Glucosinolates (e.g. sulforaphane and indoles)
- Iron, zinc, iodine and other trace minerals
- Vitamin K

Anti-cancer

Dark green vegetables provide cancer protection. Brassicas, especially broccoli, are rich in sulforaphane and indoles (phytochemicals called glucosinolates), which help neutralize cancer-causing substances in the body. Research has shown that the more cruciferous vegetables you eat, the lower your chances of developing bowel cancer.

Healthy heart

Scientists believe that eating greens is good for your heart, thanks to the presence of antioxidants and a pigment in green vegetables called lutein, both of which can help prevent hardening of the arteries, a condition that may lead to heart disease. Lutein is found in brassicas, salad greens, cucumber, peas, asparagus, avocado, beans, celery and spinach.

Pregnancy

Of all the nutrients needed during pregnancy for mother's and baby's health, vitamin C, beta-carotene and calcium are particularly vital. In addition, folic acid is the most significant nutrient for a mother-to-be as it has been shown to reduce the risk of birth defects like spina bifida. About 600 mcg of folic acid daily is recommended for pregnant women and those trying to conceive – eat at least two portions a day of folic acid-rich foods like dark green leafy vegetables, beans and asparagus, and take a 400 mcg folic acid supplement.

Folic acid has other functions, too. It is an important anti-haemorrhage and is believed to help reduce the risk of bowel cancer, heart disease, stroke, dementia and osteoporosis.

choosing
& using greens

Buying top-quality ingredients is the key to good cooking and eating, as well as good nutritional content. This is especially true for green vegetables. Since many nutrients break down on contact with heat and air, the freshness of the produce and the way it is cooked can alter its nutritional value.

Fresh, frozen or canned?

Vegetables picked from the garden and eaten within an hour or two are by far the best in terms of nutrients. In comparison, most of the so-called fresh vegetables in the supermarket are already several days old, and by the time they reach our table some vitamins (especially vitamin C and folic acid, which are susceptible to damage from light and heat) are reduced by as much as 70 per cent. Frozen or canned foods like peas and green beans, which are processed within hours of being picked, may actually contain more nutrients than 'fresh' produce.

Boosting the nutrient content in fresh produce

* Buy seasonal and locally grown vegetables – these will have spent less time in transit and storage and therefore lost fewer nutrients.
* Buy only healthy-looking produce – antioxidants are destroyed when air gets into fruit and vegetables through bruises or splits.
* Avoid produce that is displayed outside or in windows – heat and sunlight also destroy nutrients.
* Store vegetables in the refrigerator. Chilling reduces vitamin C deterioration in broccoli, for example, by around 40% in one week.

Raw or cooked?

Vegetables are generally considered more nutritious raw rather than cooked because the nutrients in fresh produce can be destroyed by bad cooking methods. For example, spinach boiled in water loses 45% of its vitamin C, 35% of its folic acid and at least 5% of every other nutrient. However, good cooking methods soften the tough cell walls of some vegetables enabling our bodies to better absorb certain nutrients.

Cook to minimize nutrient loss

- Boiling vegetables causes nutrients to leach out into the water, especially vitamin C which is water soluble. If you do boil, use as little water as possible and eat vegetables when slightly crunchy. Use the cooking water in gravy or sauces.
- Minimal water and cooking time mean less nutrient loss, so microwaving and pressure-cooking, followed by steaming, stir-frying and baking, are the best ways to cook vegetables.
- Use lids on saucepans to contain the heat and help reduce cooking time.
- Keep skins on vegetables.

Storing and preparing

Store vegetables and salad greens, unwashed, in loosely sealed plastic bags in the coldest part of the refrigerator – usually the salad drawer. To minimize nutrient loss on exposure to air, cut vegetables just before they are needed.

Prepacked vegetables might not need cleaning, but others will require washing under cold running water or swirling around in a bowl of cold water to allow the sand and grit typically found on leafy greens to settle.

Some leafy green vegetables have thick stems that are tough and woody – remove them by folding the leaves in half and ripping out the stems. If necessary, peel away the age-toughened skin on Swiss chard stems, the ends of asparagus spears and the thick stems of broccoli before cooking.

Other green vegetables benefit from brief blanching before use. The smaller you cut vegetables, the quicker they will cook – often within 1–5 minutes. Even cabbage, spring greens and Brussels should be cooked for no more than 5 minutes. This pre-empts the breaking down of the sulphurous compounds, which accounts for the bad smell associated with cooked cabbage and school dinners.

encouraging kids to eat greens

Eating fruit and vegetables is important at any age but for children it is vital. In the short term, it provides the essential nutrients required for strong healthy growth. In addition, the earlier we start eating a nourishing diet the greater our foundation for a long life and a vigorous old age. As many parents know, however, it can be hard to get kids to eat fruit and vegetables, especially green ones.

Why kids hate veggies

Toddlers have more tastebuds than adults – on their tongues, in the lining of their cheeks and the roof of their mouths – which means that they taste fruit and vegetables very differently from the rest of us. Dark green and cruciferous vegetables taste bitter to toddlers and trying to force feed them their greens can be disastrous. It can set off a negative reaction to all fruits and vegetables.

   As children get older, peer pressure and advertising play a part in what they will and won't eat. They commonly go through a stage of refusing to eat certain foods, and green vegetables are often top of the hate list. With such passing fads, yesterday's hated vegetable may equally become tomorrow's favourite. Don't pay your children too much attention when they won't eat something. Instead comment positively when they eat the right foods. It is important not to force the issue, making the meal table a battleground. Research has shown that children need to be introduced to new food up to eight times before they will accept it, so just keep trying.

Pro-veggie tactics

You may find you need to employ a few clever strategies at mealtimes to encourage your children to eat their greens.

Make vegetables fun

Rather than simply telling your children that they must eat their greens, stimulate their interest by making them understand what vegetables are, where they come from and how they are good for us. Involve them in growing vegetables, planning the menu, cooking and preparing the vegetables.

Visual appeal

Present vegetables in interesting ways – as finger foods, cut into attractive shapes, or griddled for a stripy effect. Serve younger children vegetable mash funny faces, using peas, beans and broccoli pieces for facial features and shredded cabbage or watercress for hair.

Disguise

If your child suddenly decides that he or she hates all green vegetables, use subterfuge! Blend vegetables into tomato-based pasta sauces, soups and stews; conceal them in pancake fillings or in cheese sauce with pasta; mash hated greens into potatoes; or serve with dairy foods to disguise the more bitter tastes, for example by mixing spinach with ricotta cheese. Incorporate vegetables within the main meal – for example, a vegetable pizza – rather than serving children vegetables as an accompaniment that can be left, ignored, on the plate.

Set an example

Set your child an example by eating healthy foods yourself. After all, if you are eating French fries with your steak, why should your child eat green beans?

Copy-cat tactics

Peer pressure is very powerful and children will often copy each other's eating habits. Use a child who eats his or her greens as a good role model. Invite them to supper and praise their eating habits in front of your child.

Bribery

Reward your children for eating their greens with stickers, gold stars or some other treat, but never with unhealthy foods like biscuits or sweets.

Limit distractions

Keep the dessert out of sight until the main course is finished.

greens
at a glance: a–z

Green vegetables are versatile, low fat, high fibre and packed with a range of powerful nutrients.

Asparagus

Asparagus starts to lose its flavour as soon as it is cut – the tips are the best part. White asparagus reflects a different growing technique that protects the asparagus from the light.
Source of: B vitamins (including folic acid), vitamin C, calcium, phosphorus, magnesium, potassium, iron, copper, lutein, glucosinolates, glutathione (which has antioxidant and anticarcinogenic properties).
Good for: strengthening veins and capillaries; positive liver function; preventing cancer; controlling blood pressure; stimulating the appetite. Has a diuretic effect.

Beans, broad (fava beans)

The pods of very young broad beans are edible and simply require trimming at both ends. They can be eaten raw. Old broad beans have very tough skins, which need removing before or after cooking.
Source of: protein, vitamin C, potassium, phosphorus, calcium, iron.
Good for: providing energy; healthy brain function; fighting cholesterol; controlling blood pressure; managing diabetes.

Beans, green

French bean, haricot vert, bobby bean, runner bean, string bean, snap bean, wax bean and yard long bean (Chinese long bean) are all familiar names of green beans. They need trimming at both ends and some varieties need 'stringing' to remove the fibrous indigestible 'string' that runs down the bean pod's seam. Green beans are also available cut and frozen or canned.
Source of: protein, vitamin C, beta-carotene, folic acid, calcium, potassium, phosphorus.
Good for: energy provision; fighting cholesterol; controlling blood pressure; healthy gastrointestinal system; managing heart disease, gout and rheumatism; providing a diuretic effect.

Broccoli

Broccoli is the top green vegetable for good health. The most common varieties are green broccoli (also called sprouting broccoli and calabrese) and purple sprouting broccoli.

Source of: protein, vitamins B1, B2 and C, beta-carotene, folic acid, calcium, magnesium, phosphorus, potassium, sodium, sulphur, selenium, iron, lutein, sulforaphane and indoles.

Good for: bone health; preventing cancer (particularly bowel and rectal cancers).

Brussels sprouts

Of the brassicas, Brussels are among the highest in sulforaphane content. Cutting a cross into the end of large sprouts helps speed up the cooking process. Frozen sprouts are close to fresh ones in nutritional value.

Source of: vitamin C, beta-carotene, vitamin K, folic acid, potassium, phosphorus, iron, lutein, sulforaphane and indoles.

Good for: preventing stroke and cancer (particularly digestive and colorectal cancers. May also regulate oestrogen levels, thereby lowering the risk of breast cancer).

Cabbage

The many varieties include hard red and white tight-headed cabbage; green hearted cabbages like the crinkly-leaved Savoy cabbage; and Chinese cabbages such as pak choi (bok choy) and Chinese leaves (pe-tsai, or Napa cabbage). Varieties of cabbage family without a proper head, or heart, are simply known as 'greens', for example spring greens.

Source of: vitamin C, beta-carotene, folic acid, potassium, lutein, glucosinolates including sulforaphane and indoles.

Good for: general detoxification and liver function; regulating the nervous system; treating and preventing stomach ulcers, mastitis and heart disease; preventing cancer (particularly breast cancer). Like many other cruciferous vegetables, cabbages act particularly on the stomach.

Chard (Swiss chard)

Also called spinach beet, chard has oval-shaped, glossy dark green leaves with edible white, pink or red (as in ruby chard) fleshy stalks and ribs. It is a good substitute for spinach.

Source of: beta-carotene, vitamin C, B vitamins, calcium, iron, magnesium, phosphorus, potassium.

Good for: healthy skin, eyes and hair; boosting the immune system.

Endive/chicory

This is a slightly bitter-tasting plant with ragged-edged leaves. Varieties include the curly endive or frisée and the Batavian endive, also known as escarole. It is used mainly in salads but can also be baked, steamed and sautéed.

Source of: beta-carotene, folic acid, vitamin C, calcium, potassium, phosphorus.

Good for: dealing with anaemia and stress; maintaining a healthy colon; preventing osteoporosis.

Kale

The dark green leaves – crinkly or smooth-leaved according to variety – are usually cooked although young leaves can be used raw in salads. Kale can be used as a substitute for spinach. It has more available calcium than milk.

Source of: beta-carotene, folic acid, vitamin C, vitamin E, calcium, potassium, manganese, iron, sulforaphane and indoles.

Good for: boosting the immune system; eye health; protecting against cancer.

Lettuce (dark green/red varieties)

The darker green the leaves, the more nutritious the salad green. Romaine lettuce, for example, has seven to eight times as much beta-carotene as iceberg lettuce.

Source of: beta-carotene, vitamin C, folic acid, calcium, potassium, phosphorus, lutein.

Good for: keeping the colon healthy; general health and nutrient provision; eyesight; insomnia (also contains sleep-inducing ingredients); preventing cancer.

Peas

Garden peas are available fresh, frozen, canned or dried. Sugar snaps and mangetouts (also called snow peas and sugar peas) are varieties of peas with tender edible pods. One cup of garden peas provides more protein than an egg.

Source of: protein, vitamin C, beta-carotene, folic acid, calcium, phosphorus, potassium, iron, zinc, the carotenoids lutein and zeaxanthin.

Good for: eyesight; cholesterol; diabetes control; enriching the blood; dealing with fatigue.

Pepper, green

A green pepper is an unripe red or yellow pepper. Green pepper can be eaten raw or cooked. It provides twice as much vitamin C as a citrus fruit.

Source of: vitamin C, beta-carotene, potassium, lycopene.

Good for: preventing cancer (particularly lung and prostate cancers); heart disease; boosting the immune system.

Rocket (arugula)

Another cruciferous vegetable, rocket is a salad green with long delicate-looking leaves and a sharp mustard flavour. It is used both raw and cooked.

Source of: beta-carotene, vitamin C, folic acid, calcium, indoles.

Good for: preventing cancer.

Salad greens

This broad category includes endive, lettuce, rocket, baby spinach and watercress (see separate entries), as well as dandelion leaves, lamb's lettuce (also called corn salad and mache), mizuna, nettle leaves, sorrel and vine leaves.

Source of: beta-carotene, vitamin C, folic acid, calcium, lutein.

Good for: dealing with constipation and irritation of the intestinal mucous membranes; nervous system function.

Seaweed

Freshly cut seaweed needs thorough washing in fresh water before cooking. Dried seaweeds can be found in oriental stores and healthfood shops, and need rehydrating in water before use. Dulse is a purply-red European seaweed. Wakame, kombu, hijiki and nori are widely used in Japanese cooking.

Source of: iron, iodine, calcium, magnesium, phytoestrogens.

Good for: bone health; hormone balancing; heart health; speeding the metabolism.

Spinach

Spinach has dark green leaves, which are usually lightly cooked although young leaves can be used raw in salads. Its iron content is not as high as once thought but it is a powerful antioxidant. Its oxalic acid, a substance that blocks the body's absorption of calcium and iron, makes spinach unsuitable for anyone with gastritis, hepatic or renal disease.

Source of: folic acid, beta-carotene, vitamins B, C, D and K, calcium, potassium, sodium, phosphorus, magnesium, manganese, iron, lutein, quercetin (a phytochemical with antioxidant properties).

Good for: bone health (prevents osteoporosis); detoxification; energy; eyesight (main preventor of macular degeneration); anaemia; constipation.

Watercress

Another cruciferous vegetable, watercress has small, dark green leaves on long thin stalks with a hot peppery flavour.

Source of: vitamin C, beta-carotene, calcium, iron, lutein, chlorophyll.

Good for: improving blood; raising energy levels; dealing with muscle cramps and night blindness; treating lung cancer.

chapter one

super
soups & starters

spinach & broccoli soup

Spinach and broccoli are both excellent sources of folate or folic acid, the B vitamin that is vital for the healthy development of unborn babies.

olive oil
2 tablespoons

butter
50 g (2 oz or 4 tablespoons)

onion
1, diced

garlic
1 clove, crushed

potatoes
2, peeled and cubed

broccoli
250 g (8 oz), chopped

fresh spinach
300 g (10 oz), washed and chopped

chicken or vegetable stock
750 ml (1¼ pints or 3 cups)

Gorgonzola cheese
125 g (4 oz), crumbled into small pieces

lemon juice
2 tablespoons

freshly grated nutmeg
½ teaspoon

salt and pepper

pine nuts, to garnish
75 g (3 oz), toasted

1 Heat the oil and butter in a saucepan, add the onion and garlic, and sauté for 3 minutes.

2 Add the chopped potatoes, broccoli, spinach and stock, bring to the boil and simmer for 15 minutes.

3 This soup can be puréed or left with chunky pieces. Add the Gorgonzola to the soup with the lemon juice, nutmeg and salt and pepper to taste. Garnish with the toasted pine nuts and serve with warm, crusty bread.

preparation time: 10 minutes
cooking time: 20 minutes

serves 4

olive oil

1 tablespoon

rindless unsmoked streaky bacon

50 g (2 oz), finely chopped

onion

1, chopped

celery

1 stick, thinly sliced

Brussels sprouts

375 g (12 oz), trimmed and chopped

water

900 ml (1½ pints or 3⅔ cups)

potatoes

375 g (12 oz), peeled and cubed

marjoram

1 teaspoon finely chopped,
   or ½ teaspoon dried

freshly grated nutmeg

1 pinch, or to taste

egg yolk

1

milk

4 tablespoons

salt and white pepper

serves 4–6

1 Heat the oil in a heavy-bottomed saucepan. Add the bacon and cook over a moderate heat until golden. Add the onion and celery and cook, covered, over a moderate heat for 5 minutes, stirring frequently. Add the Brussels sprouts and cook for 5–8 minutes more.

2 Add the water, potatoes, marjoram and nutmeg. Cook, uncovered, for about 30 minutes over a moderate heat. Add salt and pepper to taste.

3 In a blender or food processor, purée the mixture until smooth, in batches if necessary. Transfer to a clean saucepan.

4 In a small bowl blend the egg yolk with the milk. Bring the soup to simmering point and reheat thoroughly. then stir in the egg and milk mixture. Do not allow the soup to boil or else it will curdle.

preparation time: 15 minutes
cooking time: 45 minutes

Brussels sprouts are rich in sulforaphane, a compound that is thought to help neutralize cancer-causing substances.

Brussels sprout soup

1 Drain and rinse the soaked beans and put them in a saucepan with 125 g (4 oz) of the chorizo in one piece, the rosemary, bouquet garni and cold water. Bring to the boil and boil rapidly for 10 minutes, then simmer gently, covered, for 1–1½ hours, until the beans are tender.

2 Heat the oil in a frying pan and fry the onion, garlic, red pepper and cayenne for 5 minutes. Dice the remaining chorizo, add to the pan and fry for a further 5 minutes.

3 Stir the onion mixture into the cooked beans with the cabbage and salt and pepper. Bring to the boil and cook for 20 minutes. Add the parsley, adjust the seasoning to taste and spoon into warmed bowls. Drizzle with olive oil and serve immediately with crusty bread.

preparation time: 15 minutes, plus overnight soaking
cooking time: 2–2½ hours

dried broad beans
175 g (6 oz), soaked overnight in cold water

chorizo sausage
250 g (8 oz)

fresh rosemary
2 sprigs

bouquet garni
1

cold water
1.8 litres (3 pints or 7¼ cups)

olive oil
2 tablespoons, plus extra for drizzling

onion
1, chopped

garlic
2 cloves, crushed

red pepper
1 small, cored, deseeded and chopped

cayenne pepper
1 pinch

Savoy cabbage
250 g (8 oz), shredded

fresh parsley
1 tablespoon chopped

salt and pepper

serves 4

Among its many benefits, cabbage provides a high level of potassium, which has been shown to reduce the incidence of stroke.

bean& cabbage soup

minted
green pea
soup

Peas are a great source of a pigment called lutein, which benefits eyesight and is also believed to help prevent hardening of the arteries.

olive or sunflower oil
1 tablespoon

onion
1, chopped

celery
2 sticks, chopped

hot paprika
1–2 teaspoons

chicken or vegetable stock
1 litre (1¾ pints or 4 cups)

fresh or frozen peas
750 g (1½ lb)

fresh mint
3 sprigs

lime juice
1 tablespoon

crème fraîche or single cream
150 ml (¼ pint or ⅔ cup)

salt and pepper

to serve:

a little hot paprika

fresh mint sprigs

croûtons

serves 6

1 Heat the oil in a large pan and fry the onion and celery until soft but not brown. Stir in the paprika and fry for a few minutes. Bring the stock to the boil in another pan then add the peas, mint and lime juice. Bring back to the boil, then reduce the heat and simmer for 15–20 minutes until the peas are tender. If using frozen peas, cook for only 5–8 minutes. Do not overcook the peas or the soup will lose its bright green colour.

2 When the peas are soft, purée the soup in a blender or food processor until smooth. Alternatively, strain the soup through a wire mesh strainer. Return the purée to the pan, bring to the boil, and season with salt and pepper to taste. Remove from the heat and stir in two-thirds of the crème fraîche or cream, then add a little extra stock if necessary, to give the desired consistency. Warm through gently.

3 Serve the soup in shallow bowls with a spoonful of the remaining crème fraîche in the centre of each bowl. Sprinkle a little paprika on top and garnish each with a sprig of mint and croûtons.

preparation time: 20 minutes
cooking time: 45 minutes

dried haricot or
cannellini beans

50 g (2 oz), soaked overnight

olive oil

3 tablespoons

garlic

2 cloves, crushed

celery

1 stick, finely chopped

leeks

2, cut into rounds

tomatoes

3, skinned and chopped

fresh flat leaf
parsley

3 tablespoons, chopped

fresh basil

1 tablespoon, chopped

fresh chives

1 tablespoon chopped

French beans

125 g (4 oz), trimmed and cut into
2.5 cm (1 inch) pieces

asparagus

125 g (4 oz), trimmed and cut into
2.5 cm (1 inch) pieces

fresh or frozen
broad beans

150 g (5 oz), defrosted if frozen, grey
skins removed

fresh or frozen peas

125 g (4 oz)

boiling water, or
chicken or vegetable
stock

1 litre (1¾ pints or 4 cups)

long-grain rice

75 g (3 oz)

fresh spinach

175 g (6 oz), washed

salt and pepper

Parmesan cheese,
to serve

50 g (2 oz), freshly grated

red pesto:

garlic

2 cloves, chopped

fresh basil leaves

25 g (1 oz)

pine nuts

3 tablespoons

sun-dried tomatoes
in oil

8, drained

extra virgin olive oil

125 ml (4 fl oz or ½ cup)

Parmesan cheese

25 g (1 oz), freshly grated

serves 4–6

1 Drain and rinse the dried beans, place in a saucepan and cover with cold water. Bring to the boil, reduce the heat and simmer for 45–60 minutes or until tender. Remove from the heat and set aside in their cooking liquid.

2 Meanwhile, make the pesto. Place the garlic, basil, pine nuts and sun-dried tomatoes in a blender or food processor and process until finely chopped. With the motor running, gradually add the oil in a thin stream until it is amalgamated. Scrape the mixture into a bowl, stir in the grated Parmesan cheese and season to taste with salt and pepper.

3 Heat the oil in a large saucepan, add the garlic, celery and leeks and cook gently for 5–10 minutes until softened. Add the tomatoes with half of the herbs, season with salt and pepper and cook until the tomatoes become pulp-like, about 12–15 minutes.

4 Add the French beans, asparagus and broad beans and peas if using fresh. Cook for 1–2 minutes, then add the water or stock. Bring to the boil and boil rapidly for 10 minutes. Add the rice, the cooked haricot or cannellini beans and their cooking liquid and the spinach (and the broad beans and peas if using frozen) and cook for 10 minutes. Adjust the seasoning to taste and stir in the remaining herbs. Serve with a spoonful of pesto in each bowl of soup and sprinkled with the grated Parmesan.

preparation time: 35 minutes, plus overnight soaking
cooking time: 1¾–2 hours

Green vegetables and pulses contain the fibre that is needed to maintain a healthy digestive tract.

minestrone with red pesto

broccoli
& Cheddar cheese
soup

Thanks to its high vitamin and mineral content, **broccoli** provides good protection against heart disease, cancer and respiratory infections.

1 Melt the butter or margarine in a large saucepan. Add the onion and broccoli stalks and cook, covered, for 5 minutes over a moderate heat. Stir frequently.

2 Add the broccoli florets, potato and vegetable stock to the pan. Bring the mixture to the boil. Cook, partially covered, for 5 minutes. Remove six or more florets for a garnish and set aside. Season the mixture with salt and pepper and continue to cook over a moderate heat for 20 minutes, or until all the vegetables are soft.

3 Purée the mixture in a blender or food processor until smooth, in batches if necessary. Transfer to a clean saucepan and add the cream, lemon juice, Worcestershire sauce and a few drops of Tabasco. Simmer for 3–5 minutes. Do not allow to boil or the soup will curdle. Just before serving, stir in the grated cheese and garnish each portion with the reserved florets and sprigs of watercress.

preparation time: 25 minutes
cooking time: 45 minutes

butter or margarine
50 g (2 oz or 4 tablespoons)

onion
1, chopped

broccoli
1 kg (2 lb), divided into small florets and stalks peeled and cut into pieces

potato
1 large, peeled and quartered

vegetable stock
1.5 litres (2½ pints or 6 cups)

single cream
125 ml (4 fl oz or ½ cup)

lemon juice
1 tablespoon

Worcestershire sauce
1 teaspoon

Tabasco sauce
a few drops, or to taste

mature Cheddar cheese
125 g (4 oz), grated

salt and pepper

watercress sprigs, to garnish

serves 6

young asparagus spears
500 g (1 lb), trimmed

pine nuts
50 g (2 oz), toasted

Parmesan cheese
25 g (1 oz), shaved into slivers

salt and pepper

balsamic vinegar dressing:

balsamic vinegar
2 tablespoons

garlic
1–2 cloves, crushed

tomatoes
375 g (12 oz), skinned, deseeded and finely chopped

olive oil
5 tablespoons

serves 4

1 To make the dressing, mix the balsamic vinegar, garlic, tomatoes and olive oil in a bowl and set aside.

2 Heat a griddle pan, add the asparagus in a single layer and cook for 5 minutes over a medium heat, turning constantly.

3 Divide the asparagus between four warmed plates. Spoon over the balsamic vinegar dressing, top with the pine nuts and Parmesan shavings. Season and serve at once.

preparation time: 15 minutes
cooking time: 5 minutes

Asparagus strengthens the veins and capillaries and promotes healthy liver function.

hot asparagus with balsamic vinegar dressing

1 Line a 23 x 30 cm (9 x 12 inch) Swiss roll tin with greaseproof paper and brush lightly with some of the butter. Squeeze all the liquid from the cooked spinach; chop finely or purée. Beat in the remaining butter, the egg yolks and salt and pepper to taste. Whisk the egg whites until just stiff then fold into the spinach mixture. Turn into the prepared tin and cook in a preheated oven, 190°C/375°F/Gas 5, for 10–15 minutes.

2 To make the filling, beat the cream cheese and spring onions together. Mix the broccoli and tomatoes into the cream cheese and season well.

3 Turn the cooked roulade out on to clean greaseproof paper. Carefully peel off the lining paper and trim the edges. Spread the filling evenly over three-quarters of the roulade and roll up from the unfilled end. Wrap paper tightly over the roulade and chill for 30 minutes, before serving sliced, with a few salad leaves.

preparation time: 30 minutes, plus chilling
cooking time: 15–20 minutes
oven temperature: 190°C/375°F/Gas 5

butter
50 g (2 oz or 4 tablespoons), softened

fresh spinach
375 g (12 oz), washed and cooked

eggs
3, separated

salt and pepper

filling:

cream cheese
375 g (12 oz)

spring onions
1 bunch, chopped

broccoli
175 g (6 oz), trimmed, blanched, and finely chopped

tomatoes
4, skinned, deseeded and finely chopped

serves 4

Spinach helps to guard against cataracts and age-related macular degeneration, which is a common cause of blindness in the over-55s.

spinach
roulade

broad bean,
pear & pecorino
crostini

Broad beans are a valuable energy-providing food. They have plenty of dietary fibre and are a good source of iron.

Italian sfilatino or small thin French baguette
1, sliced into thin rounds

extra virgin olive oil, for brushing and mixing

fresh broad beans
250 g (8 oz), shelled

ripe pear
1 small, peeled, cored and finely chopped

balsamic or sherry vinegar
1 drop

pecorino, salted ricotta or feta cheese
125 g (4 oz), cut into small cubes

salt and pepper

serves 6

1 Brush the slices of bread with olive oil and arrange on a baking sheet. Bake in a preheated oven, 190°C/375°F/Gas 5, for about 10 minutes, until golden and crisp.

2 Meanwhile, blanch the beans for 3 minutes in boiling water. Drain and refresh in cold water. Pop the beans out of their skins. Mash them roughly using a fork, moistening with a little olive oil. Season with salt and pepper.

3 Mix the chopped pear with the balsamic or sherry vinegar. Stir in the cubes of cheese.

4 Spread each crostini with a mound of bean purée and top with a spoonful of the pear and cheese mixture. Serve immediately.

preparation time: 20 minutes
cooking time: 10 minutes
oven temperature: 190°C/375°F/Gas 5

leek & spinach
filo triangles

Spinach is packed with fibre, and just one cup provides one-fifth of our daily iron requirement.

1 If using fresh spinach, wash and pick over it to remove any tough central stalks. Shake off surplus water.

2 Heat half of the butter in a large saucepan and fry the onion, garlic and leek until soft but not coloured. Add the spinach and stir to combine. Cover the pan tightly with greaseproof paper and a lid and cook over a moderate heat for 5–8 minutes until the spinach has wilted and is tender and all the liquid has evaporated. Shake the pan occasionally to prevent it from sticking and burning.

3 Squeeze the spinach mixture to remove any excess moisture, leave to cool, then stir in the feta and ricotta, nutmeg, pepper and beaten egg.

4 Melt the remaining butter and work with 1 sheet of pastry at a time, brushing each one with butter before peeling it off the pile. If you are using the smaller filo sheets, fold each one in half lengthways and place 1 heaped tablespoon of the spinach mixture on one of the short ends. Fold the left corner over the filling and continue folding until you have a pastry triangle

Making filo pastry is long and complicated so ready-made filo, now widely available, is generally used. Once exposed to the air, it quickly dries out and becomes brittle, so work with one sheet of pastry at a time, keeping the rest covered with clingfilm and a damp cloth.

fresh or frozen spinach

250 g (8 oz) fresh, or 125 g (4 oz) frozen, defrosted

butter

75 g (3 oz or 6 tablespoons)

onion

65 g (2½ oz), finely chopped

garlic

2 cloves, finely chopped

leek

75 g (3 oz), thinly sliced

feta cheese

40 g (1½ oz), crumbled

ricotta cheese

40 g (1½) oz

freshly grated nutmeg

1 pinch

egg

1 small, beaten

fresh or frozen filo pastry

14 sheets fresh, each 31 x 18 cm (12½ x 7 inches), or 6 sheets frozen, each 46 x 30 cm (17½ x 12 inches), defrosted

pepper

chervil or flat leaf parsley sprigs, to garnish

fromage frais or thick natural yogurt, to serve

with a small flap to tuck underneath. Brush with a little more butter and place on an oiled baking sheet. Repeat to make 14 triangles. If you are using the large sheets of filo, put two sheets on top of each other then cut into five 8 cm (3½ inch) strips, each 30 cm (12 inches) long. Brush with butter, fill and roll in the same way to form triangles. Repeat to make 15 triangles.

5 Bake in a preheated oven, 190°C/375°F/Gas 5, for 25–35 minutes until golden brown. Garnish with chervil or parsley sprigs and serve warm or at room temperature, with fromage frais or thick natural yogurt.

preparation time: 25 minutes
cooking time: 35–45 minutes
oven temperature:
190°C/375°F/Gas 5

serves 7
(makes 14–15 triangles)

1 If using vine leaves in brine, drain and rinse in a colander under cold running water. Place in a bowl, pour boiling water over the leaves and leave to soak for 20 minutes. This removes excess salt from the brine. Rinse again and drain well. If using fresh leaves, make them more pliable by blanching them in boiling water for 30 seconds. Remove and rinse under cold water. Drain well.

2 Lightly toast the breadcrumbs in a dry pan over a medium heat, shaking the pan frequently. Add the crushed garlic and 1 tablespoon of the olive oil and cook for 1–2 minutes, or until the garlic has softened. Remove from the heat.

3 Toast the hazelnuts or pine nuts in another dry, hot pan, shaking the pan frequently. Roughly chop the nuts and stir into the cooling breadcrumbs.

4 Lay out four vine leaves, vein sides up. Place a cheese round on each. Sprinkle the breadcrumb mixture, then the thyme leaves, on top. Wrap each vine leaf around the cheese, followed by a second vine leaf then a bay leaf. Secure with string or a cocktail stick.

5 Place the parcels in an ovenproof dish and drizzle the remaining olive oil over them. Cook on the middle shelf of a preheated oven, 200°C/400°F/Gas 6, for 8–10 minutes, or until the leaves are just beginning to brown. Serve at once with crusty bread and a few salad leaves.

preparation time: 10 minutes, plus soaking
cooking time: 15 minutes
oven temperature: 200°C/400°F/Gas 6

tip:
If goat's cheese crottins are not available, use chunks of feta instead and warm in the oven for 5 minutes. Unwrap and serve on rustic bread with an extra drizzle of olive oil.

Vine leaves and herbs are widely used in the healthy, low-cholesterol diet typical of the Mediterranean region.

goat's cheese
baked in vine & bay leaves

fresh vine leaves or vine leaves in brine
8 large

white breadcrumbs
4 tablespoons

garlic
1 clove, crushed

olive oil
6 tablespoons

whole hazelnuts or pine nuts
6–8

goat's cheese
4 small rounds (crottins)

thyme leaves
1 teaspoon

bay leaves
4 large

serves 4

scallops
with ginger
& asparagus

Asparagus is another green vegetable believed to offer protection against cancer.

fresh scallops

12

spring onions

2, thinly sliced

lime

1, rind finely grated and juice of ½ lime extracted

ginger cordial

1 tablespoon

extra virgin olive oil

2 tablespoons, plus extra for drizzling

thin asparagus spears

250 g (8 oz), trimmed

mixed salad greens

a few

chervil

a few sprigs

salt and pepper

serves 4

1 Wash the scallops and pat dry. Cut each one in half and place them in a bowl.

2 Mix together the spring onions, lime rind, ginger cordial and half the oil and season to taste with salt and pepper. Pour over the scallops and set aside to marinate for 15 minutes.

3 Meanwhile, steam the asparagus spears for 5–8 minutes, or until tender. Toss with the remaining oil and the lime juice. Season to taste with salt and pepper and keep warm.

4 Heat a large nonstick frying pan until hot. Add the scallops and sauté for 1 minute on each side, or until golden and just cooked through. Add the marinade juices.

5 Arrange the asparagus spears, salad greens and chervil on four plates. Top with the scallops and any pan juices and serve.

preparation time: 10 minutes, plus marinating
cooking time: 10 minutes

chapter two

green
light
bites

eggs florentine

Like many other green vegetables, **spinach** is believed to reduce the risk of specific cancers, particularly skin and stomach cancer.

1 Melt half the butter in a large saucepan. Add the spinach with just the water that clings to the rinsed leaves. Cover tightly and sweat until the leaves have wilted, the spinach is tender and any liquid has evaporated. Transfer the spinach to a large sieve or colander and squeeze out any liquid that remains. Return to the pan, add the tomatoes and season with nutmeg, salt and pepper.

2 Grease six 175 ml (6 fl oz or ⅙ quart) gratin dishes with the remaining butter. Divide the spinach among the dishes, making a well in the centre of each for an egg and leaving a 1 cm (½ inch) space between the spinach and the rim of the dish.

3 Break an egg into the centre of each gratin dish and dust with salt and pepper. Mix together the crème fraîche and cream. Spoon evenly over the eggs and sprinkle with the grated Cheddar and Parmesan.

4 Set the gratin dishes on a heavy baking sheet and bake in a preheated oven, 220°C/425°F/Gas 7, for about 10–12 minutes, until the whites of the eggs are set but the yolks are still runny.

5 Remove the dishes from the oven and place under a preheated grill until the topping is bubbling and the cheese golden brown. Serve immediately.

preparation time: 15 minutes
cooking time: 15–20 minutes
oven temperature:
220°C/425°F/Gas 7

butter
40 g (1½ oz or 3 tablespoons)

fresh spinach
1 kg (2 lb), washed

tomatoes
2 large, diced

eggs
6 large

crème fraîche
150 ml (¼ pint or ⅔ cup)

double cream
50 ml (2 fl oz or ¼ cup)

Cheddar cheese
40 g (1½ oz), grated

Parmesan cheese
40 g (1½ oz), freshly grated

freshly grated nutmeg, salt and pepper

serves 6

extra virgin olive oil
6 tablespoons

onion
1, chopped

garlic
4 cloves, crushed

dried chilli flakes
½ teaspoon

chard leaves
500 g (1 lb)

chickpeas
400 g (13 oz) can, drained and rinsed

eggs
6

fresh parsley
2 tablespoons chopped

salt and pepper

serves 8

1 Heat 4 tablespoons of the oil in a large heavy-bottomed nonstick frying pan. Add the onion, garlic and chilli flakes and fry gently for 10 minutes until softened and lightly golden.

2 Meanwhile, wash and dry the chard and cut away and discard the thick white central stalk. Shred the leaves. Stir the chard and chickpeas into the onion mixture and cook gently for 5 minutes.

3 Beat the eggs in a bowl, add the parsley and season with salt and pepper. Stir in the chickpea mixture.

4 Wipe out the pan, then add the remaining oil. Pour in the egg and chickpea mixture and cook over a low heat for 10 minutes until the tortilla is almost cooked through.

5 Carefully slide the tortilla on to a large plate, invert the pan over the tortilla and then flip it back into the pan.

6 Return the pan to the heat for 5 minutes until the tortilla is cooked through. Leave it to cool to room temperature then serve cut into wedges or squares.

preparation time: 15 minutes
cooking time: 30–40 minutes

As well as being packed with a huge amount of beta-carotene, chard is rich in calcium, iron, magnesium, phosphorus and potassium, all important minerals for body health.

chard & chickpea tortilla

1 Heat most of the olive oil in a frying pan with a heatproof handle, add the onions and garlic, and sauté for 3 minutes; do not brown.

2 Beat the eggs in a large bowl; season well with salt and pepper, then add the chopped spinach and crumble in three-quarters of the ricotta. Add the pine nuts and olives and mix well. Add the onions and garlic, and mix again.

3 Heat the remaining oil in the frying pan, pour in the spinach mixture and cook for 5 minutes.

4 Sprinkle with the remaining ricotta, season with salt and pepper, and place the pan in a preheated oven, 200°C/400°F/Gas 6, for 15 minutes.

5 When cooked, the frittata should be set and golden on top. To serve, ease a knife around the edge and underneath and slide the frittata on to a large plate. Serve hot or cold.

preparation time: 10 minutes
cooking time: 25 minutes
oven temperature:
200°C/400°F/Gas 6

olive oil
2 tablespoons

onions
2, finely sliced

garlic
1 clove, crushed

eggs
5

fresh spinach
500 g (1 lb), washed and chopped

ricotta cheese
175 g (6 oz)

pine nuts
50 g (2 oz)

black olives
25 g (1 oz), pitted and chopped

salt and pepper

serves 4–6

Thanks to its calcium, magnesium and manganese content, spinach is a great choice for those suffering from osteoarthritis.

spinach
& ricotta
frittata

fresh pea & tomato frittata

Frozen **peas** are as good, if not better, a source as fresh ones for vitamin C, an antioxidant nutrient with infinite health-giving benefits.

fresh peas
125 g (4 oz)

extra virgin olive oil
2 tablespoons

spring onions
1 bunch, sliced

garlic
1 clove, crushed

cherry tomatoes
125 g (4 oz), halved

eggs
6

fresh mint
2 tablespoons chopped

pea shoots (optional)
1 handful

salt and pepper

serves 4

1 Cook the peas in a saucepan of lightly salted boiling water for 3 minutes. Drain and refresh under cold water.

2 Heat the oil in a nonstick frying pan and sauté the spring onions and garlic for 2 minutes, then add the tomatoes and peas.

3 Beat the eggs in a bowl with the mint and season with salt and pepper. Swirl the egg mixture into the frying pan, scatter over the pea shoots, if using, and cook over a medium heat for 3–4 minutes, or until almost set.

4 Transfer the pan to a preheated grill and cook for 2–3 minutes longer, or until lightly browned and cooked through. Cool slightly and serve in wedges with rocket and Parmesan shavings, if desired.

preparation time: 10 minutes
cooking time: 12 minutes

spinach
&chickpea
quiche

Spinach contains energy-giving iron and lots of folic acid, a nutrient proven to reduce the risk of birth defects.

1 To make the pastry, sift the flour into a bowl with the salt. Rub in the diced butter until the mixture resembles fine breadcrumbs. Gradually work in enough of the cold water to form a soft dough. Knead until smooth on a lightly floured surface. Wrap in clingfilm and chill for 30 minutes.

2 Roll out the pastry on a lightly floured surface and use it to line a greased deep 20 cm (8 inch) fluted flan tin. Prick the base and chill for 20 minutes. Line the pastry case with foil and fill with dried beans, then bake in a preheated oven at 200°C/400°F/Gas 6 for 10 minutes. Remove the foil and beans and bake the pastry case for a further 10–12 minutes, until the pastry is crisp and golden.

3 Meanwhile, prepare the filling. Place the spinach in a large saucepan with just the water that clings to the rinsed leaves. Heat gently for 3–4 minutes until the spinach wilts. Drain well, squeeze out the excess liquid, chop finely and set aside.

4 Heat the oil in a saucepan, add the onion, garlic and turmeric, and fry for 5 minutes. Stir in the chickpeas and spinach, then remove from the heat. Spread over the bottom of the cooked pastry case.

5 Beat together the eggs, cream, nutmeg and salt and pepper, and pour into the pastry case. Bake for 35–40 minutes until firm and golden.

preparation time: 25 minutes, plus chilling
cooking time: about 1 hour
oven temperature: 200°C/400°F/Gas 6

fresh spinach
175 g (6 oz), washed

extra virgin olive oil
2 tablespoons

onion
1 small, thinly sliced

garlic
2 cloves, crushed

ground turmeric
1 teaspoon

chickpeas
200 g (7 oz) can, drained and rinsed

eggs
2, lightly beaten

single cream
200 ml (7 fl oz or scant 1 cup)

freshly grated nutmeg, salt and pepper

shortcrust pastry:
plain flour
175g (6 oz or 1½ cups), plus extra for dusting

salt
½ teaspoon

butter
75 g (3 oz or 6 tablespoons), diced

cold water
2–3 tablespoons

serves 6–8

extra virgin olive oil
4 tablespoons, plus extra for brushing

onion
1, finely chopped

garlic
1 clove, crushed

fresh root ginger
2 teaspoons grated

button mushrooms
175 g (6 oz), sliced

dried dulse or nori seaweed
175 g (6 oz), cut into small pieces

dark soy sauce
1 tablespoon

lemon juice
1 tablespoon

fresh coriander
2 tablespoons chopped

fresh white breadcrumbs
50 g (2 oz)

pine nuts
50 g (2 oz)

sesame seeds
2 tablespoons

fresh or frozen filo pastry
12 sheets, defrosted if frozen

pepper

serves 4–6

1 Heat half the oil and fry the onion, garlic and ginger gently for 5 minutes. Add the mushrooms and fry for 5 minutes, stirring. Add the seaweed to the pan with the soy sauce, lemon juice and coriander. Stir over a low heat until the seaweed is soft.

2 In another pan, heat the remaining oil and stir-fry the breadcrumbs, pine nuts and sesame seeds for 4–5 minutes. Take one sheet of filo pastry and trim to fit an oiled 20 x 30 cm (8 x 12 inch) roasting tin. Press into the base and brush with oil.

3 Scatter over 2 teaspoons of the breadcrumb mixture. Repeat with five more sheets of pastry and half the breadcrumb mixture. Spread over the seaweed mixture then repeat the layers, ending with a layer of pastry.

4 Brush liberally with oil, mark into four or six portions and bake in a preheated oven, 190°C/375°F/Gas 5, for 30 minutes until crisp and golden.

preparation time: 25 minutes
cooking time: 50 minutes
oven temperature:
190°C/375°F/Gas 5

Several varieties of seaweed are edible. Most are rich in useful vitamins and minerals – particularly iron, required for the formation of red blood cells, and iodine, which is necessary for efficient functioning of the thyroid gland.

seaweed filo pie

spinach
crêpes
with asparagus

Both **spinach** and **asparagus** are sources of folate, or folic acid, which is thought to help reduce the risk of bowel cancer, and has a beneficial effect on our mood.

1 First make the béchamel sauce. Put the milk, onion and bay leaf in a saucepan and heat until just boiling. Remove from the heat and set aside for 20 minutes to infuse. Strain the milk and reserve.

2 To make the crêpes, first cook the spinach leaves with just the water that clings to the rinsed leaves in a covered heavy-bottomed saucepan for 2 minutes or until wilted. Drain thoroughly, pressing out any excess water. Chop finely. Put the flour and salt in a bowl and make a well in the centre. Pour the egg and some of the milk into the well.

Whisk the liquid, gradually incorporating the flour to make a smooth paste. Whisk in the remaining milk and the chopped spinach, then pour the batter into a measuring cup with a pouring spout. Allow to rest, if desired.

3 Put a little oil or butter in an 18 cm (7 inch) crêpe pan or heavy-bottomed frying pan and heat until it starts to smoke. Pour off the excess and pour a little batter into the pan, tilting it until the base is coated with a thin layer. Cook for 1–2 minutes until the underside begins to turn golden.

4 Flip the crêpe with a spatula and cook for a further 30–45 seconds until it is golden on the second side. Slide the crêpe out of the pan and keep warm. Make another seven crêpes in the same way, greasing the pan each time as necessary. Keep the cooked crêpes warm.

5 Continue with the béchamel sauce. Melt the butter in a saucepan, stir in the flour, and cook over a low heat for 1 minute. Remove from the heat and beat in the infused milk, a little at a time, until blended. Return to a low heat and stir constantly until thickened.

thick asparagus spears
24, trimmed

mild white Cheddar cheese
50 g (2 oz), grated

spinach crêpes:

fresh spinach
250 g (8 oz), washed and trimmed

plain flour
150 g (5 oz or 1¼ cups)

salt
1 pinch

egg
1, lightly beaten

milk
300 ml (½ pint or 1¼ cups)

vegetable oil or butter, for greasing

béchamel sauce:

milk
300 ml (½ pint or 1¼ cups)

onion
1 small, roughly chopped

bay leaf
1

butter
25 g (1 oz or 2 tablespoons)

plain flour
25 g (1 oz or ¼ cup)

salt and pepper

Bring to a gentle boil, stirring, then simmer for 2 minutes. Season with salt and pepper.

6 Blanch the asparagus spears in a large saucepan of lightly salted boiling water for 2 minutes. Drain, refresh under cold running water and pat dry with kitchen paper.

7 Place three asparagus spears on each crêpe and roll them up. Place the crêpes seam-side down in a lightly greased, shallow baking dish. Pour the béchamel sauce over the top and sprinkle with the grated cheese.

8 Place the dish under a preheated grill and cook for 8–10 minutes until bubbling and golden. Serve at once.

preparation time: 20 minutes, plus resting batter and infusing milk
cooking time: 35–45 minutes

serves 4

spinach&
egg muffins with
mustard hollandaise

Spinach contains considerable levels of sight-saving lutein.

1 Place the spinach and nutmeg in a saucepan and add the water. Set aside while making the hollandaise.

2 Next, make the sauce: place the lemon juice, egg yolks and mustard in a heatproof bowl set over a saucepan of gently simmering water. Add a piece of the butter and whisk until the butter has melted into the sauce. Continue whisking in the butter, a piece at a time, until the sauce is thickened and smooth. This takes about 5 minutes. If the sauce becomes too thick, whisk in 1 tablespoon hot water. Keep the sauce warm over the simmering water until ready to use.

3 Toast the muffins and keep warm. Place the vinegar in a saucepan with plenty of hot water, bring to a gentle rolling boil and break the eggs one at a time into the pan to poach them. Meanwhile, cover the spinach pan with a lid and cook for about 1 minute until the spinach has wilted.

4 Transfer the toasted muffins to four serving plates, pile them up with the spinach, then the poached eggs, and finally the hollandaise sauce. Serve immediately.

preparation time: 10 minutes
cooking time: 10 minutes

fresh baby spinach
200 g (7 oz), washed

freshly grated nutmeg
1 pinch

water
1 tablespoon

lemon juice
1 tablespoon

egg yolks
2

coarse grain mustard
1 tablespoon

lightly salted butter
40 g (1½ oz or 3 tablespoons), diced

English muffins
4, split

vinegar
1 tablespoon

eggs
4

serves 4

Ingredients

vegetable oil
3 tablespoons

garlic
1 clove, crushed

watercress
750 g (1½ lb), washed and drained

mirin (rice wine)
1 tablespoon

tamari or soy sauce
2 tablespoons

coarsely ground black pepper
¼ teaspoon

freshly grated nutmeg

Thai or oriental basil leaves
15 g (½ oz), torn

serves 4

1 Heat the oil in a large saucepan, add the crushed garlic and cook gently for 30–60 seconds until it is soft but not brown.

2 Add the watercress, mirin and tamari or soy sauce and stir-fry over a high heat for 1–2 minutes or until just wilted.

3 Season the watercress with the pepper and add grated nutmeg to taste. Add the torn basil leaves, then remove the pan from the heat. Serve with cooked brown rice and more soy sauce, if liked.

preparation time: 5 minutes
cooking time: 5 minutes

Only cook watercress just long enough for the leaves to wilt to retain as much of its vitamin C and beta-carotene as possible. Watercress also has a high iodine content, useful for stimulating the thyroid.

wilted watercress with garlic & nutmeg

1 If the endive is discoloured, trim a thin slice from the root end, and remove any damaged or brown leaves. If only the tips of the leaves have developed a brown edge, trim them with scissors. Cut each endive head in half lengthways and remove the central core, leaving the head intact.

2 Melt the butter in a large frying pan, add the endives cut-side down, and sprinkle with the lemon juice. Fry until browning, turning several times and taking care to keep the heads together.

3 Transfer the endive to a 2–2½ litre (3¼–4 pint or 2–2½ quart) gratin dish and scatter with the fried bacon. Mix together the mustard, cream and two-thirds of the cheese, season with salt and pepper and pour over the endive. Scatter over the remaining cheese and place in a preheated oven, 200–220°C/400–425°F/Gas 6–7, for about 20 minutes until bubbling and golden. Finish the browning under a hot grill, if necessary. Garnish with chervil sprigs and serve.

preparation time:
10–15 minutes
cooking time: 25–30 minutes
oven temperature:
200–220°C/400–425°F/
Gas 6–7

endive
8 heads

butter
25 g (1 oz or 2 tablespoons)

lemon juice
from 1 large lemon

lightly smoked bacon
8 large thin slices, rinded, chopped and fried until crisp

Dijon mustard
2 tablespoons

single cream
300 ml (½ pint or 1¼ cups)

Swiss or mature Cheddar cheese
65 g (2½ oz), grated

salt and pepper

chervil sprigs, to garnish

serves 4

Endive is full of folic acid, lack of which during pregnancy can result in spina bifida in the baby.

endive
& smoked bacon gratin

braised soya beans with spinach & shiitake mushrooms

A source of magnesium and calcium, spinach is superb for strengthening bones and teeth.

soya beans
175 g (6 oz), soaked overnight, drained and rinsed

extra virgin olive oil
3 tablespoons

garlic
1 clove, chopped

fresh root ginger
1 teaspoon grated

red chillies
2, deseeded and chopped

shiitake mushrooms
125 g (4 oz), sliced

tomatoes
4, ripe, skinned, deseeded and chopped

dark soy sauce
2 tablespoons

dry sherry
2 tablespoons

fresh spinach
250 g (8 oz), washed and shredded

serves 4

1 Place the soaked beans in a saucepan with plenty of cold water. Bring to the boil and boil rapidly for 10 minutes, then reduce the heat, cover and simmer for 1 hour, or until the beans are tender. Drain, reserving 150 ml (¼ pint or ⅔ cup) of the cooking liquid.

2 Heat the oil in a large frying pan. Add the garlic, ginger and chillies and fry for 3 minutes. Add the mushrooms and fry for a further 5 minutes until tender.

3 Add the tomatoes, beans, reserved cooking liquid, soy sauce and sherry and bring to the boil. Cover and simmer for 15 minutes.

4 Stir in the spinach and heat through for 2–3 minutes until the spinach has wilted. Serve at once.

preparation time: 15 minutes, plus overnight soaking
cooking time: 1¾ hours

spinach
with Japanese
sesame dressing

This very simple recipe retains as much of the iron, vitamin C and beta-carotene in the spinach as possible.

1 Put the washed spinach leaves in a large bowl or saucepan, pour boiling water over the leaves and blanch for 1 minute. Drain immediately and refresh under cold water. Drain well, then chop the leaves roughly.

2 Put the sesame seeds and caster sugar in a blender or small food processor and blend to a coarse purée, or use a pestle or mortar. Add the soy sauce, a little at a time, until it becomes a smooth paste. Add the mirin and blend well.

3 Pour the dressing over the spinach and toss together well. Spoon the spinach into mounds in small serving bowls and top with the toasted sesame seeds. Serve with plain boiled brown or red rice.

preparation time: 10 minutes
cooking time: 1 minute

fresh spinach
750 g (1½ lb), washed, tough stalks removed

sesame seeds
6 tablespoons

golden caster sugar
1½ teaspoons

light soy sauce
3½ tablespoons

mirin (rice wine)
1 tablespoon

sesame seeds, to garnish
2 tablespoons, toasted

serves 4–6

asparagus
500 g (1 lb)

rocket or other green leaves
125 g (4 oz)

spring onions
2, finely sliced

radishes
4, thinly sliced

salt and pepper

tarragon and lemon dressing:

tarragon vinegar
2 tablespoons

finely grated lemon rind
from 1 lemon

Dijon mustard
¼ teaspoon

sugar
1 pinch

fresh tarragon
1 tablespoon chopped

olive oil
5 tablespoons

to garnish:

chopped herbs (e.g. dill, tarragon, parsley, chervil)

thin strips of lemon rind

serves 4

1 Trim the ends of each asparagus stalk by cutting across at a sharp angle. Make the cut just where the lovely bright green colour starts to fade into a dull green.

2 To make the dressing, put all the dressing ingredients in a screw-top jar and shake well.

3 Heat a griddle pan. Place the asparagus on the griddle in a single layer and cook for about 5 minutes, turning occasionally. The asparagus should be tender when pierced with the tip of a sharp knife, and lightly browned in patches. Transfer to a shallow dish and season to taste with salt and pepper. Pour over the dressing and toss gently. Set aside to cool for 5 minutes.

4 Arrange the rocket or green leaves on a platter, sprinkle the spring onions and radishes over the top and arrange the asparagus in the middle of the leaves. Garnish with chopped herbs and thin strips of lemon rind. Serve with bread or as an accompaniment to a main dish.

**preparation time: 15 minutes
cooking time: 5 minutes**

Rich in fibre, folic acid and vitamin C, asparagus also has anti-cancer properties thanks to its detoxifying glucosinolates.

asparagus
with tarragon
& lemon dressing

chapter three

salad
greens

1 Slice each pear quarter in half. Heat a griddle pan. Place the slices of pear on the griddle and cook for 1 minute on each side. Remove from the pan and sprinkle with the lemon juice.

2 Pile the spinach on a large platter or 4 serving plates and arrange the griddled pears on top. Sprinkle with the walnuts and crumbled Stilton and spoon the walnut oil over the salad. Serve immediately.

preparation time: 15 minutes
cooking time: 7 minutes

pears
4, quartered and cored

lemon juice
4 tablespoons

fresh baby spinach
250 g (8 oz), washed

walnuts
4, chopped

blue Stilton cheese
250 g (8 oz), crumbled

walnut oil
4 tablespoons

serves 4

The strong green colour in spinach comes from chlorophyll, which offers many health benefits. These include wound healing, combating anaemia, improving heart action and reducing abnormally high blood pressure.

griddled pear & spinach salad

orecchiette,
broad bean &
pecorino salad

Broad beans are packed with potassium, the mineral responsible for regulating the body's fluid levels, including blood pressure.

fresh or frozen broad beans
750 g (1½ lb) fresh young beans in the pod, or 250 g (8 oz) frozen, defrosted

orecchiette or similar short pasta shapes
500 g (1 lb)

extra virgin olive oil
5 tablespoons

pecorino cheese
75 g (3 oz), grated

pitted black olives
50 g (2 oz), finely chopped

flat leaf parsley
5 tablespoons chopped

balsamic vinegar
1 tablespoon

salt and pepper

serves 4

1 Shell the broad beans, if fresh. Bring a saucepan of lightly salted water to the boil, add the fresh or defrosted frozen beans and blanch for 1 minute. Drain, refresh under cold water, then drain again. Pop the beans out of their shells.

2 Cook the pasta in plenty of lightly salted boiling water, with a dash of oil, for 12—15 minutes or according to packet instructions, until just tender. Drain the pasta in a colander, refresh under cold water and drain thoroughly.

3 Tip the pasta into a large salad bowl and add the remaining ingredients. Toss well, add plenty of pepper and serve.

preparation time: 15 minutes
cooking time: 15 minutes

tomato & green bean salad

Green beans are rich in fibre and are a marvellous source of co-enzyme Q10, a nutrient involved in the production of energy in the body's cells.

mixed red and yellow baby tomatoes, plum if possible
250 g (8 oz)

thin green beans
250 g (8 oz), trimmed

fresh mint
1 handful, chopped

garlic
1 clove, crushed

extra virgin olive oil
4 tablespoons

balsamic vinegar
1 tablespoon

salt and pepper

serves 4

1 Cut the baby tomatoes in half and place in a large bowl.

2 Cook the green beans in a saucepan of lightly salted boiling water for 2 minutes, then drain well and place in the bowl with the tomatoes.

3 Add the chopped mint, garlic, olive oil and balsamic vinegar. Season with salt and pepper and mix well. Serve warm or cold.

preparation time: 10 minutes
cooking time: 2 minutes

pomegranate
1

watercress
1 bunch, broken into sprigs

oranges
4

rosewater or orange flower water
1 teaspoon

olive oil
5 tablespoons

raspberry or white wine vinegar
1 tablespoon

pink peppercorns in brine
½ teaspoon, drained

sea salt flakes

serves 4

1 Break open the pomegranate and remove the seeds, discarding the bitter yellow pith. Place the seeds in a large bowl with the watercress.

2 Finely grate the rind from 2 of the oranges and set aside. Peel and segment all the oranges and carefully remove the membrane around each segment, catching any juices in the bowl containing the pomegranate and watercress. Place the orange segments in the bowl with the watercress.

3 In a separate bowl, combine the rosewater or orange flower water, olive oil, vinegar, pink peppercorns and reserved grated orange rind. Mix well, pour over the salad, season with a few sea salt flakes and serve as an accompaniment to barbecued meat.

preparation time: 20 minutes

Eat watercress raw to increase its potent health benefits, due to high levels of vitamins (especially beta-carotene and vitamin C) and minerals.

watercress & pomegranate salad

1 To make the vinaigrette, place all the ingredients in a screw-top jar and shake well. Measure out 75 ml (3 fl oz or generous ⅓ cup) for use in this recipe. (The leftover vinaigrette can be stored for up to one week in the refrigerator in a screw-top jar.)

2 Heat the walnuts in a dry pan over a medium heat for 1–2 minutes until slightly toasted. Set aside.

3 Whisk together the olive vinaigrette and pitted olives in a small bowl.

4 Mix together the chickpeas, pepper, carrot and onion in a medium bowl. Toss with 3 tablespoons of the vinaigrette.

5 Toss the spinach and other salad leaves with the remaining vinaigrette. Transfer to a large serving bowl, top the leaves with the vegetable mixture and sprinkle with the toasted walnuts.

preparation time: 20 minutes
cooking time: 1–2 minutes

walnuts
75 g (3 oz), chopped

pitted olives
1 tablespoon

chickpeas
400 g (13 oz) can, drained and rinsed

red pepper
1, cored, deseeded and thinly sliced

carrot
1 large, cut into matchsticks

red onion
1 small, thinly sliced

fresh baby spinach
4 handfuls, washed

green salad leaves
4 handfuls

olive vinaigrette:

balsamic vinegar
50 ml (2 fl oz or ¼ cup)

lime juice
50 ml (2 fl oz or ¼ cup)

garlic
1 clove, crushed

black olives
2 pitted and chopped

Dijon mustard
½ tablespoon

sugar
1 small pinch

serves 6

Spinach and salad greens provide all-round health benefits that include healthy bones, blood and eyes.

mediterranean
vegetable
& walnut salad

oriental-style coleslaw

Raw cabbage is good for the digestive system: for detoxifying as well as for soothing stomach upsets and indigestion.

white radish
1, cut into long, thin strips

carrot
1 large, cut into long, thin strips

Chinese cabbage (such as pak choi)
½, shredded

red cabbage
¼, shredded

spring onions
2, cut into long, thin strips

mangetout
18, cut lengthways into thin strips

fresh spinach
50 g (2 oz), washed and shredded

fresh or dried figs
50 g (2 oz), cut lengthways into quarters

flaked almonds
75 g (3 oz)

dressing:

sesame seeds
2 tablespoons

fresh root ginger
3 teaspoons grated

sugar
1 teaspoon

sherry or rice wine vinegar
3 tablespoons

peanut oil
2 teaspoons

soy sauce
2 teaspoons

sesame oil (optional)
a few drops

serves 6

1 Place all the salad ingredients in a large serving bowl and toss them well to combine.

2 To make the dressing, heat the sesame seeds in a small, dry saucepan over a medium heat, shaking the pan frequently for 2–3 minutes until toasted.

3 Stir in the remaining dressing ingredients. Remove the pan from the heat, immediately pour the dressing over the salad. Toss to combine.

preparation time: 20 minutes
cooking time: 2–3 minutes

tip:

Vary the coleslaw recipe by substituting or adding one or more of the following ingredients: white cabbage, fennel, celery, onions, apples, orange, sunflower seeds, pumpkin seeds, dried fruit such as sultanas, raisins and ready-to-eat apricots, walnuts, pine nuts, garlic, fresh herbs.

summer salad
with mixed seeds

Asparagus and avocados are fine sources of lutein which can help protect against heart disease. To retain all the vitamins and minerals, make the salad and the dressing just before serving.

1 Add the asparagus spears to a saucepan of boiling water. Cook for 2–3 minutes. They will still be crunchy. Drain well and refresh in cold water.

2 Cut the avocados in half and remove the stones. Dice the flesh and add it immediately to the lemon juice, to prevent it from turning brown.

3 Remove the avocados from the lemon juice, reserving any juice, and add to a bowl with the asparagus. Add the toasted sesame seeds and linseeds and the assorted herb leaves.

4 Put the toasted pumpkin seeds in a coffee grinder or blender and grind until finely chopped. Mix the ground pumpkin seeds with the olive oil, any reserved lemon juice, the finely chopped basil, salt and pepper. Whiz in the blender or pound in a mortar. Drizzle the dressing over the salad and serve immediately.

preparation time: 20 minutes
cooking time: 5 minutes

thin asparagus spears
250 g (8 oz), trimmed

avocados
2, ripe but firm

lemon juice
2 tablespoons

sesame seeds
1 tablespoon, toasted

linseeds
1½ teaspoons

assorted herb leaves (e.g. rocket, basil, flat leaf parsley, chervil)

pumpkin seeds
1 tablespoon, toasted

olive oil
5 tablespoons

basil leaves
15 g (½ oz), finely chopped

salt and pepper

serves 4

spring cabbage

250 g (8 oz)

light vinaigrette
dressing

50 ml (2 fl oz or ¼ cup)

light soy sauce

1 teaspoon

celery

3 sticks, sliced

spring onions

4, chopped

red pepper

1, cored, deseeded and diced

red pepper strips,
to garnish

serves 6

1 Pick over the cabbage leaves carefully, discarding any that are blemished. Shred the cabbage.

2 Combine the vinaigrette dressing with the soy sauce. Put the spring cabbage in a bowl with the dressing, mix thoroughly and leave to marinate for 1 hour.

3 Add the remaining ingredients and mix thoroughly. Serve, garnished with pepper strips.

preparation time: 15 minutes, plus marinating

tip:

Make this salad the same day that you buy the spring cabbage, as the leaves soon become limp.

Cabbage is rich in valuable minerals, including calcium, magnesium, potassium, phosphorus and iodine.

spring cabbage
& pepper salad

1 Cook the pasta in plenty of lightly salted boiling water, with a dash of oil, for 8–12 minutes or according to packet instructions, until just tender. Drain the pasta, rinse in a colander under cold running water, and drain again. Transfer to a bowl.

2 While the pasta is cooking, blanch the asparagus and sugar snap peas in a saucepan of boiling water for 2 minutes, then drain and refresh under cold water and drain again. Add to the bowl of pasta, along with the carrot, spring onions and red peppers.

3 Heat the sesame and sunflower oils in a small heavy-bottomed saucepan. Add the ginger and sesame seeds and cook for 30–60 seconds until the seeds start to pop. Remove the pan from the heat, stir in the soy sauce, and season with salt and pepper, to taste.

4 Pour the dressing over the pasta and mix thoroughly.

preparation time: 15 minutes
cooking-time: 10–12 minutes

caserecce twists or other dried pasta
300 g (10 oz)

asparagus tips
125 g (4 oz), cut in half widthways

sugar snap peas
1 large handful, trimmed

carrot
1 large, cut into 2.5 cm (1 inch) matchsticks

spring onions
4, cut into 2.5 cm (1 inch) matchsticks

red peppers
2, cored, deseeded and cut into 2.5 cm (1 inch) matchsticks

sesame oil
2 tablespoons

sunflower oil
2 tablespoons

fresh root ginger
2.5 cm (1 inch), peeled and finely shredded

sesame seeds
2 teaspoons

soy sauce
50 ml (2 fl oz or ¼ cup)

salt and pepper

serves 4

Peas and asparagus contain fibre, folic acid and vitamin C. Asparagus is good for blood pressure and peas help lower cholesterol.

oriental pasta **salad**

spinach, artichoke & bacon salad

with a warm dressing

Jerusalem artichokes
4 small, scrubbed and cut into 5 mm (¼ inch) thick slices

walnut oil
2 tablespoons

smoked pancetta
8 slices

walnuts
40 g (1½ oz)

extra virgin olive oil
4–6 tablespoons

garlic
1 clove, crushed

balsamic vinegar
2 tablespoons

fresh baby spinach
125 g (4 oz), washed

watercress
50 g (2 oz)

assorted herb leaves (e.g. basil, chervil, mint, parsley)
4 tablespoons chopped

salt and pepper

serves 4

Both **spinach** and **watercress** are powerful detoxifiers.

1 Toss the Jerusalem artichokes with the walnut oil in a roasting tin or ovenproof dish and roast in a preheated oven, 200°C/400°F/Gas 6, for 20 minutes, turning halfway through the cooking time.

2 Meanwhile, grill the pancetta until it is crisp and then break it into bite-sized pieces. Dry-fry the walnuts, stirring constantly, until evenly browned. Set aside.

3 Heat 1 tablespoon of the olive oil in a small pan and sauté the garlic for 1 minute, until lightly golden. Add the vinegar and remaining olive oil, season to taste with salt and pepper, and keep warm.

4 Place the spinach leaves and watercress in a large bowl and add the pancetta, toasted walnuts, artichokes and herbs and mix well. Arrange the salad on serving plates and drizzle over the warm dressing. Serve immediately.

preparation time: 10 minutes
cooking time: 20 minutes
**oven temperature:
200°C/400°F/Gas 6**

bacon, spinach & blue cheese salad

Research confirms that eating **greens** is the right choice for your heart.

rindless smoked back bacon
3 rashers, chopped

pine nuts
25 g (1 oz)

fresh baby spinach
225 g (7½ oz), washed

Gorgonzola cheese
50 g (2 oz), cubed

cherry tomatoes
12, halved

dressing:

wholegrain mustard
1 teaspoon

balsamic vinegar
2 tablespoons

clear honey
1 teaspoon

serves 4

1 Fry the bacon in a nonstick frying pan until crisp. Add the pine nuts and continue to cook for 1–2 minutes until the nuts begin to brown.

2 Toss together the spinach, Gorgonzola and tomatoes, then stir these into the bacon and pine nuts. Place the salad in a serving bowl.

3 Mix together the dressing ingredients and drizzle over the salad. Serve with crusty bread.

preparation time: 10 minutes
cooking time: 5 minutes

olive oil
1 tablespoon

onion
1, sliced

garlic
1 clove, crushed

chicken livers
250 g (8 oz), halved

balsamic vinegar
2 tablespoons

tomatoes
3, chopped

black-eyed beans
400 g (13 oz) can, drained and rinsed

fresh baby spinach
225 g (7½ oz), washed

serves 4

1 Heat the oil in a pan, add the onion and garlic and fry for 2 minutes.

2 Add the chicken livers and fry for 3–4 minutes until just cooked through.

3 Stir in the balsamic vinegar, tomatoes and beans and heat through for a further 2 minutes. Toss through the spinach and serve with crusty bread.

preparation time: 10 minutes
cooking time: 10 minutes

Spinach is an outstanding source of iron. Used raw as a salad ingredient, it provides maximum nutritional value.

chicken liver, black-eyed bean & spinach salad

chapter four

umpteen greens
for pasta & rice

1 Trim any tough, fibrous ends from the asparagus spears and cut the stalks in half. Lay the thicker stalk ends in a frying pan, cover with boiling water and cook for 1 minute. Add the asparagus tips and cook for a further minute. Drain and set aside.

2 Put the mascarpone in a bowl and crumble in the saffron. Add the garlic, tarragon and a little salt and pepper and blend until smooth.

3 Heat 2 tablespoons of the remaining oil in a frying pan and quickly fry the mushrooms until they are beginning to brown.

4 Lay six sheets in a lightly greased large, shallow, ovenproof dish. Reserve 12 asparagus tips and scatter the rest of the asparagus over the pasta. Dot with half of the mascarpone. Cover with another layer of lasagne and scatter with the mushrooms. Dot with the remaining mascarpone and place the reserved asparagus on top.

5 Sprinkle with the breadcrumbs and a little salt and pepper. Drizzle with the remaining olive oil. Bake in a preheated oven at 200°C/400°F/Gas 6 for 15 minutes until heated through. Serve immediately.

preparation time: 20 minutes
cooking time: 25 minutes
oven temperature:
200°C/400°F/Gas 6

Asparagus contains vitamins C, K and potassium. It is also a dependable source of folic acid, essential for brain and nerve development and function.

asparagus
& mushroom
lasagne

asparagus
500 g (1 lb)

mascarpone cheese
150 g (5 oz)

saffron threads
1 teaspoon

garlic
3 cloves, crushed

fresh tarragon
3 tablespoons chopped

olive oil
4 tablespoons

fresh ready-to-use lasagne
12 sheets

mixed wild mushrooms or chestnut mushrooms
300 g (10 oz), sliced if large

coarse breadcrumbs
40 g (1½ oz)

salt and pepper

serves 6

olive oil
2 tablespoons

onion
1, chopped

garlic
1 clove, crushed

fresh spinach
750 g (1½ lb), washed and chopped

freshly grated
nutmeg
1 pinch

fresh ready-to-use
lasagne
8 sheets

cooked ham
250 g (8 oz), chopped into large chunks

buffalo mozzarella
125 g (4 oz), thinly sliced

fontina cheese
125 g (4 oz), grated

salt and pepper

serves 4

pasta bake
with spinach
& ham

One of the most nutritious leafy green vegetables, **spinach** protects and strengthens the body.

1 Heat the olive oil in a saucepan, add the onion and garlic, and sauté for 3 minutes.

2 Add the spinach and mix well. Cook for 2 minutes over a moderate heat, just so that the spinach starts to wilt. Add nutmeg to taste, and season with salt and pepper.

3 Lightly oil a large, shallow baking dish. Place a layer of lasagne at the bottom, followed by a layer of spinach, then ham, and then a layer of mozzarella. Repeat until all the ingredients are used, finishing with lasagne and the grated fontina cheese.

4 Place the dish at the top of a preheated oven, 200°C/400°F/Gas 6, and bake for 15 minutes until golden brown and bubbling.

preparation time:
15–20 minutes
cooking time: 20 minutes
oven temperature
200°C/400°F/Gas 6

pasta
primavera

Green vegetables are a wonderful source of powerful antioxidants, as well as the minerals iron, calcium and zinc.

olive oil
2 tablespoons

garlic
1 clove, crushed

shallots
2, chopped

shelled peas
125 g (4 oz)

young broad beans
125 g (4 oz), shelled and grey skins removed

asparagus
125 g (4 oz), trimmed and cut into 5 cm (2 inch) lengths

fresh spinach
125 g (4 oz), washed and chopped

tagliatelle
300 g (10 oz)

whipping cream
125 ml (4 fl oz or ½ cup)

Parmesan cheese
75 g (3 oz), freshly grated

fresh mint
1 handful, chopped

salt and pepper

serves 4

1 Heat the oil in a saucepan, add the garlic and shallots, and sauté for 3 minutes. Add the peas, broad beans, asparagus and spinach to the shallot mixture. Stir well and cook for 2 minutes.

2 Meanwhile, cook the tagliatelle in a large saucepan of boiling water for 3 minutes if fresh and 7 minutes if dried, or according to packet instructions. Stir the pasta occasionally while it is cooking.

3 Stir the cream into the vegetables, mix well and simmer for 3 minutes.

4 Drain the tagliatelle thoroughly, then add the pasta to the vegetable sauce and season well with salt and pepper. Add the Parmesan and mint and toss well using two wooden spoons. Serve at once.

preparation time:
10–15 minutes
cooking time: 10 minutes

fresh baby spinach
500 g (1 lb), washed

freshly grated nutmeg
1 pinch

goat's cheese
125 g (4 oz), roughly chopped

low-fat crème fraîche
150 ml (¼ pint or ⅔ cup)

Dijon mustard
2 teaspoons

fresh wholemeal pasta
500 g (1 lb)

pine nuts
75 g (3 oz), toasted

fresh parsley
1 tablespoon chopped

Parmesan cheese
2 tablespoons, freshly grated

salt and pepper

serves 4

1 Blanch the spinach leaves in boiling water for 1 minute. Drain the leaves, squeezing out any excess water and roughly chop. Mix the spinach with the grated nutmeg, goat's cheese, crème fraîche and mustard.

2 Cook the pasta in plenty of lightly salted boiling water for 4–5 minutes or according to packet instructions, until just tender. Drain well.

3 Return the hot pasta immediately to the pan and add the spinach mixture, salt, pepper and pine nuts and toss together. Add the parsley, Parmesan and a touch more grated nutmeg and serve while still piping hot.

preparation time: 10 minutes
cooking time: 6–8 minutes

Renowned for its blood-strengthening properties, spinach prevents and relieves anaemia and helps normalize blood pressure.

spinach
& goat's cheese with wholemeal
pasta

1 Place the asparagus on a baking sheet, brush generously with olive oil, and season with salt and pepper. Place under a preheated grill and cook for 8 minutes, turning as they brown.

2 Meanwhile, cook the broad beans or peas in a saucepan of lightly salted boiling water for 2 minutes.

3 Cook the pasta in a large saucepan of boiling water for 6 minutes if fresh and 10 minutes if dried, or according to packet instructions. Remove a piece and test before draining.

4 Pour the cream into the empty pasta pan over the heat, add the cooked broad beans or peas, grilled asparagus and Parmesan, and season with salt and pepper. Return the pasta to the pan, add the mint, and toss well with two wooden spoons. Serve at once.

preparation time: 10 minutes
cooking time: 18 minutes

asparagus
500 g (1 lb), trimmed and cut into 5 cm (2 inch) lengths

olive oil
4 tablespoons

broad beans or peas
250 g (8 oz)

penne
300 g (10 oz)

double cream
75 ml (3 fl oz or generous ⅓ cup)

Parmesan cheese
75 g (3 oz), freshly grated

fresh mint
4 tablespoons chopped

salt and pepper

serves 4

Choose asparagus and beans for fibre, which is essential for keeping the digestive system in order.

penne
with broad beans, asparagus & mint

charred
asparagus
with spaghetti

Chlorophyll-rich **asparagus** is good for controlling blood pressure.

thin asparagus spears
500 g (1 lb), trimmed

extra virgin olive oil
3–4 tablespoons

lemon juice
4 tablespoons

dried spaghetti
375 g (12 oz)

garlic
2 cloves, roughly chopped

dried chilli flakes
¼–½ teaspoon

basil leaves
25 g (1 oz)

Parmesan cheese
25 g (1 oz), freshly grated, plus extra to serve

salt and pepper

serves 4

1 Brush the asparagus spears with a little oil then griddle or grill until charred and tender. Toss with a little more oil, half of the lemon juice and salt and pepper and set aside.

2 Cook the spaghetti in a large saucepan of lightly salted water according to the packet instructions until *al dente*.

3 Just before the pasta is cooked, heat the remaining oil in a large frying pan or wok and sauté the garlic with a little salt for 3–4 minutes, until softened but not browned. Add the chilli flakes and asparagus and heat through.

4 Drain the pasta, reserving 4 tablespoons of the cooking liquid, and add both to the asparagus pan with the basil, the remaining lemon juice, a little pepper and the Parmesan. Serve immediately, with extra Parmesan, if liked.

preparation time: 10 minutes
cooking time: 15 minutes

spinach
& ricotta
gnocchi

The nutrients in **spinach** all play a part in strengthening the body: calcium for strong bones and teeth, iron and vitamin K for healthy blood and folic acid for the nervous system.

1 Place the spinach in a pan with just the water that clings to the rinsed leaves. Cover and cook for a few minutes until the leaves are wilted and tender. Increase the heat to drive off any remaining water. Squeeze dry and leave to cool.

2 To make the gnocchi mixture, put the spinach, ricotta, egg yolks, Parmesan, nutmeg, sage leaves and salt and pepper in a blender or food processor and work to a smooth purée.

Turn into a bowl, sift over the flour and mix to form a dough. Cover with clingfilm and leave in the refrigerator for about 15 minutes.

3 Meanwhile, prepare the chilli butter dressing. Melt the butter and gently fry the chilli in it until soft. Keep warm.

4 Using well-floured hands, take 15 g (½ oz) pieces of the gnocchi mixture and shape them into 24 small

ovals or egg shapes. As each gnocchi is made, place it on a lightly floured tray until ready to cook.

5 Bring about 3.6 litres (6 pints or 3½ quarts) lightly salted water to the boil in a large, wide pan, reduce the heat to a simmer and poach six gnocchi at a time for 4–5 minutes until they are puffy and have risen to the surface. Remove with a slotted spoon and pile into warmed individual dishes.

6 Pour over the chilli butter, sprinkle with the Parmesan cheese and shredded sage leaves and serve immediately.

preparation time:
20 minutes, plus chilling
cooking time: 20–25 minutes

fresh spinach
750 g (1½ lb), washed and trimmed

ricotta cheese
175–250 g (6–8 oz)

egg yolks
2

Parmesan cheese
50 g (2 oz), freshly grated

freshly grated nutmeg
¼ teaspoon

sage leaves
2, finely chopped

plain flour
50 g (2 oz or ½ cup), plus extra for shaping

salt and pepper

dressing:

butter
75 g (3 oz or 6 tablespoons)

red chilli
1 small, deseeded and finely chopped

to serve:
Parmesan cheese
125 g (4 oz), freshly grated

sage leaves
6–8, shredded

serves 4

1 Melt half of the butter with the olive oil in a heavy-bottomed saucepan. Add the garlic and onion and sauté gently for 5 minutes, but do not allow them to brown.

2 Add the rice and stir well to coat the grains with the butter and oil. Add the hot stock, a ladleful at a time, stirring until each addition is absorbed into the rice. Continue adding stock in this way, cooking until the rice is creamy but the grains are still firm. This should take about 20 minutes.

3 When you add the last of the stock, add the vegetables and vermouth or white wine, mix well and cook for 2 minutes.

4 Remove the pan from the heat, season the risotto with salt and pepper and add the remaining butter, the chopped parsley and Parmesan. Mix well, then cover and leave the risotto to rest for a few minutes before serving.

preparation time: 15 minutes
cooking time: 30 minutes

serves 4

Including lots of **greens** in your diet over a period of time can help strengthen both your blood and your immune system.

green vegetable risotto

butter
125 g (4 oz or 1 stick)

olive oil
1 tablespoon

garlic
1 clove, crushed

onion
1, finely diced

risotto rice
300 g (10 oz)

hot chicken or vegetable stock
1 litre (1¾ pints or 4 cups)

French beans
125 g (4 oz), trimmed and cut into 2.5 cm (1 inch) pieces

shelled peas
125 g (4 oz)

shelled broad beans, grey skins removed
125 g (4 oz)

asparagus
125 g (4 oz), trimmed and cut into 2.5 cm (1 inch) pieces

fresh baby spinach
125 g (4 oz), washed and chopped

dry vermouth or white wine
75 ml (3 fl oz or generous ⅓ cup)

fresh parsley
2 tablespoons chopped

Parmesan cheese
125 g (4 oz), freshly grated

salt and pepper

spinach & lemon risotto

Spinach is rich in vitamin K, which is vital for blood clotting as well as kidney function.

butter
125 g (4 oz or 1 stick)

olive oil
1 tablespoon

shallots
2, finely chopped

risotto rice
300 g (10 oz)

hot chicken or vegetable stock
1 litre (1¾ pints or 4 cups)

fresh spinach
500 g (1 lb), washed and chopped

lemon
1, rind grated and juice extracted

Parmesan cheese
125 g (4 oz), freshly grated

salt and pepper

grated lemon rind, to garnish (optional)

serves 4

1 Melt half of the butter with the olive oil in a saucepan, add the shallots, and sauté for 3 minutes.

2 Add the rice and stir well to coat the grains thoroughly with butter and oil. Add a ladleful of hot stock, enough to cover the rice, and stir well. Simmer gently and continue to stir as frequently as possible, adding more stock as it is absorbed.

3 Before you add the last of the stock, stir in the chopped spinach, lemon rind and juice, and season with salt and pepper. Increase the heat, stir well, then add the remaining stock and butter. Allow to cook for a few minutes, then add half of the Parmesan and mix in well. Serve garnished with the remaining Parmesan and grated lemon rind, if using.

preparation time: 10 minutes
cooking time: 25 minutes

green veg
& goat's cheese
risotto

Broccoli and spinach both provide folic acid, which promotes the production of serotonin to help ward off depression.

extra virgin olive oil
4 tablespoons

leeks
2, sliced

garlic
2 cloves, chopped

risotto rice
250 g (8 oz)

dry white wine
150 ml (¼ pint or ⅔ cup)

hot vegetable stock
1.2 litres (2 pints or 4¾ cups)

broccoli
250 g (8 oz), divided into florets

fresh baby spinach
250 g (8 oz), washed and shredded

mixed herbs (e.g. basil, chives, mint, parsley, tarragon)
25 g (1 oz), chopped

soft goat's cheese
125 g (4 oz), mashed

Parmesan cheese
50 g (2 oz), freshly grated

salt and pepper

serves 4

1 Heat the oil in a large saucepan and sauté the leeks and garlic for 5 minutes, until softened. Add the rice and stir well to coat the grains with the oil. Add the wine, bring to the boil and cook, stirring, until almost all the liquid has evaporated.

2 Gradually add the hot stock, a ladleful at a time, stirring until each addition has been absorbed into the rice. Continue adding the stock in this way, cooking until the rice is creamy but the grains are still firm. This should take about 20 minutes. Add the broccoli to the rice after 12 minutes.

3 Stir the spinach, herbs and both cheeses into the rice. Season to taste with salt and pepper and cook for a final 2 minutes until the spinach is wilted. Cover the pan and leave the risotto to rest for a few minutes before serving.

preparation time:
10–15 minutes
cooking time: 30 minutes

Ingredients

raw prawns
500 g (1 lb)

butter
125 g (4 oz or 1 stick)

onion
1, finely chopped

garlic
2 cloves, crushed

risotto rice
250 g (8 oz)

shelled peas
375 g (12 oz)

dry white wine
150 ml (¼ pint or ⅔ cup)

vegetable stock
1.5 litres (2½ pints or 6 cups)

fresh mint
4 tablespoons chopped

salt and pepper

serves 4

1 Peel the prawns, reserving the heads and shells. Devein each prawn, wash and pat dry. Wash the heads and shells and dry well.

2 Melt half the butter in a large frying pan, add the prawn heads and shells and stir-fry for 3–4 minutes, until golden. Strain the butter and return it to the pan.

3 Add a further 25 g (1 oz or 2 tablespoons) of the butter to the pan and gently fry the onion and garlic for 5 minutes until softened. Add the rice and stir the grains for 1 minute, until coated and glossy. Add the peas and then pour in the wine and boil rapidly until reduced by half.

4 Meanwhile, bring the stock to a very gentle simmer in another pan and start adding it to the rice, a ladleful at a time. Stir constantly while gradually adding the stock until the rice is creamy but still crunchy in the middle and most of the liquid has been absorbed. This takes about 20 minutes.

5 Melt the remaining butter and stir-fry the prawns for 3–4 minutes, then stir them into the rice with the pan juices and mint, and season with salt and pepper to taste. Cover the pan and leave to rest for 5 minutes. Serve hot.

preparation time: 15 minutes
cooking time: 35–40 minutes

Peas are high in fibre. A high-fibre diet will help protect against breast cancer.

pea
& prawn
risotto

1 Heat the olive oil in a large pan and fry the onion until softened. Add the crushed garlic and pancetta to the pan and fry until the pancetta is golden brown. Add the rice and stir the grains into the onion mixture to coat them in the olive oil.

2 With the pan still over a medium heat, add the dried mixed herbs and the hot stock to the rice and bring the mixture to the boil, stirring constantly. Season with salt and pepper and reduce to a simmer. Simmer for 10 minutes, stirring frequently. Add the broad beans and peas to the pan and continue to cook for a further 10 minutes.

3 Remove the pan from the heat and stir the grated fontina though the risotto. Dot the butter on top together with the grated Parmesan. Cover the pan with a lid and leave for 2–3 minutes to allow the cheese and butter to melt into the risotto.

4 Remove the lid and add the chopped mint and shredded basil and gently stir the cheese, butter and herbs through the risotto. Serve immediately with fresh basil leaves and extra shavings of Parmesan.

preparation time: 15 minutes
cooking time: 30–35 minutes

serves 4

olive oil
3 tablespoons

onion
1, finely chopped

garlic
3 cloves, crushed

pancetta
75 g (3 oz), chopped

risotto rice
250 g (8 oz)

dried mixed herbs
½ teaspoon

hot chicken or vegetable stock
900 ml (1½ pints or 3⅔ cups)

fresh or frozen broad beans
125 g (4 oz), defrosted if frozen

peas
75 g (3 oz)

fontina
75 g (3 oz), coarsely grated

butter
50 g (2 oz or 4 tablespoons)

Parmesan cheese
2 tablespoons, freshly grated, plus extra shavings to serve

fresh mint
1 tablespoon chopped

basil leaves
6–8, shredded, plus extra to serve

salt and pepper

Both broad beans and peas are useful sources of vitamin C, which is essential for general good health.

quick broad bean & pancetta risotto

spinach

& lentil pilaff

An important energy food, **spinach** is effective for improving vitality and fighting long-term fatigue.

extra virgin olive oil
2 tablespoons

onion
1, finely chopped

garlic
4 cloves, crushed

carrots
2, chopped

aubergine
1 small, cubed

ground ginger
1 teaspoon

paprika
1 teaspoon

ground coriander
1 teaspoon

ground cumin
1 teaspoon

red lentils
250 g (8 oz), rinsed

white long grain rice
250 g (8 oz)

vegetable stock
1 litre (1¾ pints or 4 cups)

fresh spinach
250 g (8 oz), washed and shredded

sesame seeds
2 tablespoons, lightly toasted

salt and pepper

serves 4

1 Heat the oil in a large heavy-bottomed saucepan. Add the onion, garlic, carrots and aubergine and fry for 5 minutes, stirring occasionally.

2 Stir the ginger, paprika, ground coriander and cumin into the pan and cook, stirring, for 1 minute then stir in the lentils and rice. When well mixed, add the stock. Bring to the boil, cover the pan and simmer gently, stirring occasionally, for 30–35 minutes until the rice and lentils are tender and the stock has been absorbed.

3 Stir in the spinach and cook for 2 minutes until it has thoroughly wilted. Season to taste with salt and pepper. Scatter with the sesame seeds.

preparation time:
15 minutes
cooking time:
about 45 minutes

wilted spring greens
with ginger, sesame & brown rice

All **cabbages** are packed with nutrients. **Spring greens** are more delicate and cook quickly; you can use **Savoy cabbage** instead. **Seaweed** is a useful source of vitamins and minerals such as vitamin K, iron, iodine, potassium, zinc and magnesium.

1 Put the brown rice in a large saucepan of boiling water with the kombu and bring to the boil. Reduce the heat a little and cook at a fast simmer for 30 minutes. When the rice is just cooked and still retains a bite, drain well (reserving some cooking water) and discard the seaweed.

2 Meanwhile, gently cook the onion in the oil in a large pan or wok until golden brown and crisp. Add the garlic and continue to cook gently for 1 minute, stirring constantly, to flavour the oil. Do not allow the garlic to burn.

3 Add the spring greens and ginger and stir-fry for 1–2 minutes or until the greens are just wilted.

4 Combine the tamari or soy sauce, sesame oil and 6 tablespoons of the reserved rice cooking water. Add to the vegetables and stir-fry for 1 minute.

5 Remove from the heat and toss the cooked rice and the wilted spring greens together. Spoon into serving bowls and top with toasted sesame seeds and black pepper. Serve immediately or chill and serve cold.

preparation time: 15 minutes
cooking time: 30 minutes

brown rice
250 g (8 oz)

dried kombu seaweed
10 cm (4 inches)

onion
1, finely chopped

olive oil
3 tablespoons

garlic
2 cloves, crushed

spring greens
325 g (11 oz), shredded

fresh root ginger
7 cm (3 inches), finely chopped

tamari or soy sauce
4 tablespoons

sesame oil
1 tablespoon

sesame seeds
2 tablespoons, toasted

freshly ground black pepper

serves 4

broccoli
500 g (1 lb), trimmed

sugar snap peas
125 g (4 oz), trimmed

mangetouts
125 g (4 oz), trimmed

red or brown rice
250 g (8 oz)

**dried kombu
seaweed (optional)**
10 cm (4 inches)

groundnut oil
3 tablespoons

garlic
2–3 cloves, crushed

soy sauce
3 tablespoons

tahini paste
1 tablespoon

sesame oil
1 tablespoon

sesame seeds
2 tablespoons, toasted

pepper

serves 4

1 Plunge the broccoli into a large saucepan of boiling water for 1 minute. Remove and refresh immediately in a bowl of cold water.

2 Blanch the sugar snap peas and mangetouts in the boiling water in the same way for 30 seconds. Remove and refresh in the bowl of cold water for 5 minutes, then drain well. Reserve the saucepan of vegetable water.

3 Add the red or brown rice to the saucepan of vegetable water with the kombu, if using, and return to the boil. Reduce the heat a little and cook at a fast simmer for 30 minutes. When the rice is just cooked and still retains a bite, drain well, reserving a little of the water, and discard the seaweed.

4 Heat the groundnut oil in a wok or large frying pan, add the garlic and cook gently, stirring constantly, for 1 minute to flavour the oil. Do not allow the garlic to burn.

5 Add the drained vegetables to the oil and stir-fry for 1–2 minutes. Mix together the soy sauce, tahini, sesame oil and 8 tablespoons of reserved vegetable water, add to the vegetables and stir-fry for a further 1 minute.

6 Remove the wok from the heat and toss the cooked red or brown rice through the vegetables. Spoon into serving bowls and top with the toasted sesame seeds and black pepper. Either serve hot immediately, or chill and serve cold.

preparation time: 15 minutes
cooking time: 35 minutes

Broccoli is brimming with cancer-fighting phytochemicals. Adding dried kombu to the rice cooking water allows the iron and other minerals in the seaweed to be absorbed by the grains.

stir-fried broccoli
with sesame seeds & red rice

1 Place the noodles in a bowl, cover with boiling water, and let stand while preparing the vegetables.

2 Heat the oil in a large saucepan. Add the onion, chilli, garlic, ginger, ground coriander, turmeric and lemon grass and sauté gently for 5 minutes.

3 Drain the noodles. Add the coconut milk and stock to the pan and bring just to a boil. Reduce the heat and stir in the spring greens or cabbage, beans, mushrooms and drained noodles. Cover and simmer for 5 minutes. Stir in the peanuts and season to taste with salt and pepper. Serve in deep bowls.

preparation time: 20 minutes
cooking time: 20 minutes

dried medium egg noodles
125 g (4 oz)

groundnut or vegetable oil
2 tablespoons

onion
1, chopped

red chilli
1, deseeded and sliced

garlic
3 cloves, sliced

fresh root ginger
5 cm (2 inches), peeled and grated

ground coriander
2 teaspoons

ground turmeric
½ teaspoon

lemon grass
1 stalk, finely sliced

coconut milk
400 g (13 oz) can

vegetable stock
250 ml (8 fl oz or 1 cup)

spring greens or cabbage
125 g (4 oz), finely shredded

runner or French beans
275 g (9 oz), trimmed and diagonally sliced

shiitake mushrooms
150 g (5 oz), sliced

unsalted, shelled peanuts
75 g (3 oz)

salt and pepper

serves 4

Containing high levels of beta-carotene, vitamins C and E, cabbage is a potent antioxidant believed to possess cancer-fighting properties. Green beans also contain vitamin C and beta carotene.

vegetable noodles
in spiced coconut milk

rice noodle
pancakes
with stir-fried vegetables

The number one green vegetable for health, broccoli is a vital source of calcium, folic acid and vitamin C.

dried wide rice noodles
175 g (6 oz)

green chilli
1, deseeded and sliced

fresh root ginger
2.5 cm (1 inch), peeled and grated

fresh coriander
3 tablespoons chopped

plain flour
2 teaspoons

oil
2 teaspoons, plus extra for frying

stir-fried vegetables:

broccoli
125 g (4 oz)

vegetable oil
2 tablespoons

onion
1 small, sliced

red pepper
1, cored, deseeded and sliced

yellow pepper
1, cored, deseeded and sliced

sugar snap peas
125 g (4 oz), halved lengthways

hoisin sauce
6 tablespoons

lime juice
1 tablespoon

salt and pepper

1 Cook the noodles in lightly salted boiling water for 3 minutes or until tender. Drain well. Transfer to a bowl, then add the chilli, ginger, coriander, flour and the oil. Mix well and set aside.

2 Thinly slice the broccoli stalks and cut the florets into small pieces. Cook the stalks in boiling water for 30 seconds, add the florets and cook for 30 seconds more. Drain.

3 Heat ther vegetable oil in a wok or large frying pan, add the onion and stir-fry for 2 minutes. Add the peppers and stir-fry for 3 minutes until softened but still retaining texture. Stir in the cooked broccoli, sugar snap peas, hoisin sauce and lime juice, season to taste with salt and pepper, and set aside.

4 Heat some oil in a frying pan to a depth of 1 cm (½ inch). Place 4 large, separate spoonfuls of the cooked noodles (half the mixture) in the oil. Pan-fry for about 5 minutes until crisp and lightly coloured. Drain the pancakes on kitchen paper. Keep warm while cooking the remaining noodle mixture in the same way.

5 Heat the vegetables through for 1 minute in the wok or frying pan. Place two pancakes on each of four serving plates and pile the stir-fried vegetables on top.

preparation time:15 minutes
cooking time: 20–25 minutes

serves 4

chapter five

green
cuisine

beef
with broccoli
& oyster sauce

Broccoli stimulates the body's production of detoxifying enzymes that fight cancer-causing chemicals in the body and inhibit tumour growth.

1 Wrap the steak in clingfilm and place it in the freezer for 1–2 hours until it is just hard.

2 Remove the steak from the freezer and unwrap it, then slice it into small rectangles. Whisk the egg white in a bowl, add the soy sauce, garlic, ginger, cornflour and sugar and whisk to mix. Add the pieces of beef, stir to coat, then leave to marinate at room temperature for about 30 minutes or until the beef has completely defrosted.

3 Heat the groundnut oil in a deep frying pan or wok until very hot but not smoking. Add about one-third of the beef rectangles and stir them so they separate. Fry for 30–60 seconds until the beef changes colour on all sides, lift out with a slotted spoon and

drain on kitchen paper. Repeat with the remaining beef. Carefully pour off all but about 2 tablespoons of the hot oil from the pan.

4 Add the broccoli florets to the pan, sprinkle with the rice wine or sherry and toss over a moderate heat for 3 minutes. Return the beef to the pan and add the oyster sauce and soy sauce. Increase the heat to high and stir-fry vigorously for 3–4 minutes or until the beef and broccoli are tender. Taste and add more soy sauce, if liked. Serve hot, drizzled with sesame oil and sprinkled with sesame seeds.

preparation time:
about 15 minutes, plus
freezing and marinating
cooking time: 15 minutes

rump steak
375 g (12 oz), in one piece, trimmed of all fat

egg white
1

soy sauce
2 tablespoons

garlic
2 cloves, crushed

fresh root ginger
2.5 cm (1 inch), peeled and grated

cornflour
1 tablespoon

sugar
1 teaspoon

groundnut oil
about 175 ml (6 fl oz or ¾ cup)

broccoli
250 g (8 oz), divided into small florets

rice wine or dry sherry
125 ml (4 fl oz or ½ cup)

oyster sauce
3 tablespoons

soy sauce
2 tablespoons, or more to taste

sesame oil

salt and pepper

sesame seeds, to garnish
2 tablespoons, toasted

serves 2–3

cumin seeds
1 tablespoon

coriander seeds
1 tablespoon

mustard seeds
1 teaspoon

**dried red chillies
(optional)**
1–2

vegetable oil
2 tablespoons

onion
1, finely chopped

lamb fillet
500 g (1 lb), cut into thin strips across
the grain

garlic
2 cloves, crushed

ground turmeric
2 teaspoons

**chicken stock or
water**
150 ml (¼ pint or ⅔ cup)

fresh spinach
175 g (6 oz), washed and shredded

salt and pepper

serves 4

1 Heat a wok until hot, add the cumin, coriander and mustard seeds, and dried chillies if using, and dry-fry over a gentle heat for 2–3 minutes or until their aroma is released. Remove from the heat and crush the spices using a mortar and pestle.

2 Return the wok to a moderate heat, add the oil and heat until hot. Add the onion and stir-fry for 2–3 minutes or until softened, taking care not to let it brown. Add the lamb strips, garlic, crushed spices and the turmeric. Increase the heat to high and stir-fry for 3–4 minutes or until the lamb is browned on all sides. Add the stock or water and salt and pepper to taste. Stir well to mix, then add the shredded spinach and toss for 30 seconds or until just beginning to wilt. Season to taste and serve at once.

**preparation time: 15 minutes
cooking time: 10–15 minutes**

Spinach is an excellent energy booster and a source of vitamin K.

spiced lamb
with
shredded spinach

1 Drain the bacon, then put in a large saucepan, cover with fresh cold water and bring to the boil. Discard the water, rinse the bacon, wash out the pan and begin again with fresh water, adding all the ingredients except the cabbage. Bring to the boil, cover the pan and simmer for 25 minutes per 500 g/1 lb.

2 Add the cabbage wedges 20–25 minutes before the end of the cooking time and continue to cook until the bacon and cabbage are tender. Remove the bacon and cabbage from the cooking liquid and drain the cabbage well. Peel the rind from the bacon and serve in slices with the cabbage wedges, accompanied by boiled potatoes and parsley sauce.

preparation time: 10–15 minutes, plus overnight soaking
cooking time: 2 hours

tip:
A 2 kg (4 lb) joint of bacon when cooked, will provide approximately 10–20 slices, depending on whether the meat is carved hot or cold, plus a 150 g (5 oz) tail piece ideal for use in a pie.

Thanks to its antibacterial properties, cabbage stimulates the immune system.

boiled
bacon &
cabbage

joint of smoked or unsmoked bacon
2 kg (4 lb), tied in a neat shape and soaked overnight in cold water

onion
1, quartered

carrots
2, quartered

celery
2 sticks, quartered

leek
1, quartered

2 bay leaves, sprig of thyme, parsley stalks and blade of mace all tied together

peppercorns
10

green tight-headed Irish cabbage
1, cut into wedges, core removed

serves 6–8

boneless chicken breasts
4, skinned

ricotta cheese
125 g (4 oz)

cooked spinach
125 g (4 oz), squeezed dry and chopped

freshly grated nutmeg
1 pinch

Parma ham
8 slices

olive oil
2 tablespoons

salt and pepper

serves 4

chicken
stuffed with
spinach
& ricotta

Bone-strengthening nutrients in spinach mean that eating it can help reduce the risk of hip fracture in the elderly.

1 Cut a long horizontal slit through the thickest part of each chicken breast without cutting right through.

2 Crumble the ricotta into a bowl. Add the chopped spinach with the grated nutmeg. Season with salt and pepper and mix well.

3 Divide the stuffing between the four chicken breasts. Wrap each one in two pieces of Parma ham, wrapping the ham around the chicken to completely enclose the meat.

4 Heat the oil in a shallow, flameproof casserole, add the chicken breasts and sauté for 4 minutes on each side, or until the ham starts to brown. Transfer the casserole to a preheated oven, 200°C/400°F/ Gas 6, and cook for 15 minutes. The ham should be browned and slightly crunchy on the outside and the chicken moist and soft.

preparation time: 10 minutes
cooking time: 25 minutes
oven temperature:
200°C/400°F/Gas 6

chicken & spinach masala

Packed with beta-carotene, vitamins C and E, spinach is an effective antioxidant, helping to strengthen the immune system.

vegetable oil
2 tablespoons

onion
1, thinly sliced

garlic
2 cloves, crushed

green chilli
1, deseeded and thinly sliced

fresh root ginger
1 teaspoon finely grated

ground coriander
1 teaspoon

ground cumin
1 teaspoon

tomatoes
200 g (7 oz) can

boneless chicken thighs
750 g (1¾ lb), skinned and cut into bite-sized chunks

crème fraîche
200 ml (7 fl oz or scant 1 cup)

fresh spinach
300 g (10 oz), washed and coarsely chopped

fresh coriander leaves
2 tablespoons chopped

salt and pepper

serves 4

1 Heat the oil in a large heavy-bottomed saucepan. Add the onion, garlic, chilli and ginger. Stir-fry for 2–3 minutes and then add the ground coriander and cumin. Stir and cook for another 1 minute.

2 Pour in the tomatoes with their juice and cook gently for 3 minutes. Increase the heat and add the chicken. Cook, stirring, until the outside of the chicken is sealed. Then stir in the crème fraîche and spinach.

3 Cover the pan and cook the chicken mixture gently for 6–8 minutes, stirring occasionally. Stir in the fresh coriander with seasoning to taste. Serve hot with naan bread or boiled basmati rice.

preparation time: 15 minutes
cooking time: 15–20 minutes

fresh root ginger
1 cm (½ inch), peeled and grated

garlic
1 small clove, crushed

dark soy sauce
1 tablespoon

tangerine syrup
1 tablespoon

mirin (rice wine)
1½ teaspoons

sugar
1 teaspoon

Chinese five-spice powder
1 pinch

chicken breast fillets
2, skinned

pak choi
2, halved

ginger salsa:

stem ginger
2.5 cm (1 inch), finely shredded

red chilli
1, deseeded and finely chopped

coriander leaves
a few, chopped, plus extra to garnish

sesame oil
1 teaspoon

lime
½, juice extracted

1 Combine the ginger, garlic, soy sauce, tangerine syrup, mirin, sugar and five-spice powder in a bowl. Place the chicken in a shallow, heatproof dish, pour in the mixture, and turn to coat. Set aside to marinate for 10 minutes.

2 Meanwhile, make the ginger salsa. Mix the stem ginger, chilli, fresh coriander, sesame oil and lime juice.

3 Place the chicken with the marinade in a bamboo steamer and cook for 8 minutes. Remove the chicken from the dish and keep warm. Steam the pak choi in the cooking juices for 2–3 minutes. Serve the chicken and pak choi with the salsa, garnished with fresh coriander.

preparation time:
10–15 minutes, plus marinating
cooking time: 11 minutes

serves 2

High in fibre, **pak choi** is a Chinese cabbage that is excellent for keeping the digestive system in the best of health.

steamed chicken with **pak choi** & ginger

1 Dry the salmon with kitchen paper, then dip it in the egg white. Mix the sesame seeds and salt and pepper to taste on a large plate. Roll the salmon in the sesame seeds and pat on the seeds all over to give a good even coating. Heat a griddle pan, lay the salmon on top and cook for about 2 minutes on each side for rare, or 5 minutes for well done.

2 Process the dressing ingredients in a blender or place in a screw-top jar and shake well to combine. Toss the watercress and frisée in the dressing and arrange on a large serving dish.

3 Slice the salmon fillet with a sharp, thin-bladed knife and arrange on top of the salad. Drain the curled spring onions, dry on kitchen paper and sprinkle over the salmon.

preparation time: 25 minutes
cooking time: 10 minutes

salmon fillet
500 g (1 lb) (middle is best)

egg whites
2, lightly beaten

white sesame seeds
1 tablespoon

black sesame seeds
1 tablespoon

watercress
2 bunches

frisée lettuce
1, divided into leaves

spring onions
4, cut into thin strips and placed in water

salt and pepper

dressing:

white wine vinegar
3 tablespoons

vegetable oil
5 tablespoons

soy sauce
1 tablespoon

sesame oil
1 tablespoon

caster sugar
1 teaspoon

fresh chives
1 bunch, chopped

Containing the antioxidants, zinc and beta-carotene, vitamins C and E, **watercress** is a great detoxifier and useful for boosting the immune system.

sesame-crusted
salmon
with
watercress salad

serves 4

tuna teriyaki with minty pea salsa

Rich in lutein, which is good for eyesight and preventing the hardening of the arteries, peas are also full of vitamin C and folic acid.

marinade:

dry sherry
4 tablespoons

soy sauce
4 tablespoons

soft dark brown sugar
2 tablespoons

garlic
2 cloves, crushed

lemon juice
1 tablespoon

sesame oil
2 tablespoons

salsa:

fresh peas
250 g (8 oz)

virgin olive oil
tablespoons

garlic
clove, crushed

fresh mint
tablespoon chopped

cucumber
cm (3 inches), finely chopped

rice vinegar
½ tablespoons

salt and pepper

1 Mix together all the marinade ingredients. Add pepper to taste and whisk until well blended. Put the tuna in a shallow dish, pour the marinade over the fish, turn to coat well, cover and leave to marinate for 2 hours or overnight.

2 To make the salsa, cook the peas in boiling water for 3 minutes. Drain well and refresh under cold running water. Put the peas in a blender or food processor with the olive oil, garlic and chopped mint and blend briefly to a very rough purée, or use a pestle and mortar.

3 Stir the cucumber into the pea purée with the vinegar, salt and pepper to taste.

4 Remove the fish from the marinade. Cook under a preheated grill for 5–6 minutes on one side then flip over and grill the second side for 2 minutes, brushing both sides with the marinade to stop the fish drying out.

5 Put any remaining marinade in a saucepan, bring to the boil and boil for 1 minute to make teriyaki sauce. Serve the hot tuna on a bed of pea salsa and pour a little of the sauce over and around the fish. Serve with lightly grilled vegetables, such as fennel or courgettes.

preparation time:
15 minutes, plus marinating
cooking time: 12 minutes

serves 4

salmon fish cakes
with spinach & poached egg

Well known for its high iron content, spinach is equally important because it contains calcium and magnesium for bone strength.

1 Cook the potatoes in a saucepan of boiling water until just done when pierced with a sharp knife. Drain well and leave to cool.

2 Either roughly chop the salmon or process it briefly in a food processor to make a coarse mince. Using a fork or the back of a wooden spoon, roughly mash the potatoes with salt and pepper. Add the minced salmon and mix together.

3 With floured hands, divide the mixture into four and shape firmly into four plump fish cakes. Coat each one in flour and refrigerate for 1 hour.

4 Heat the oil in a large frying pan until hot. Add the fish cakes and cook for 3–4 minutes on each side.

5 Shake the washed spinach leaves dry, pack them into a saucepan with just the water that clings to the rinsed leaves and cover with a lid. Heat gently for 2–3 minutes or until the spinach has just begun to wilt. Drain the spinach thoroughly and season with a little salt and pepper.

6 Poach the eggs until just cooked. Remove the fish cakes from the oil and set them on individual plates, top each one with some of the spinach and finish with a hot poached egg. Serve with lemon wedges.

**preparation time:
20 minutes, plus chilling
cooking time: 20 minutes**

**King Edward
potatoes**
250 g (8 oz), peeled and quartered

salmon fillet
300 g (10 oz), skinned and bones
   removed

plain flour
1–2 tablespoons

**sunflower or
groundnut oil**
6–8 tablespoons

fresh spinach
500 g (1 lb), washed

eggs
4

salt and pepper

**lemon wedges, to
serve**

serves 4

raw tiger prawns

600 g (1 lb 3 oz), peeled with tails left on

sesame oil

1 teaspoon

light soy sauce

2 tablespoons

honey

1 tablespoon

fresh root ginger

1 teaspoon grated

crushed garlic

1 teaspoon

lemon juice

1 tablespoon

pak choi

500 g (1 lb)

vegetable oil

2 tablespoons

salt and pepper

serves 4

1 Put the prawns in a bowl. Add the sesame oil, soy sauce, honey, ginger, garlic and lemon juice. Season and mix well, then set aside to marinate for 5–10 minutes.

2 Bring a large saucepan of water to a rolling boil. Cut the heads of pak choi in half lengthways, then blanch in the boiling water for 40–50 seconds. Drain well, cover and keep warm.

3 Heat the oil in a large wok or frying pan. Add the prawns with their marinade and stir-fry briskly for 3–4 minutes or until the prawns are pink and just cooked through.

4 Divide the pak choi among four plates. Top with the prawns and any juices from the pan. Serve at once.

preparation time: 10 minutes, plus marinating cooking time: 4–5 minutes

Like all cabbages, pak choi has detoxifying properties and is good for the liver and stomach.

sesame prawns with pak choi

1 Place the saffron in a small bowl and pour over 300 ml (½ pint or 1¼ cups) of boiling water. Leave to infuse for 10 minutes.

2 Melt the butter in a large, flameproof casserole, add the shallots or onion and garlic and cook, without browning, for 5–6 minutes until softened. Add the pancetta or bacon and cook for a further 1–2 minutes. Add the fresh peas, lettuce, 1 teaspoon of caster sugar and the saffron and its water. Cover the casserole and cook for 10–15 minutes until the peas are tender. If using frozen peas, add to the pan after 5 minutes. Season with salt and pepper to taste, and add more sugar, if necessary.

3 Meanwhile, make the breadcrumb topping. Melt the butter in a frying pan, add the breadcrumbs and cook, stirring frequently, until golden brown. Remove from the heat, leave to cool slightly, then stir in the grated cheese.

4 Beat the egg yolks in a small bowl and, when the peas are cooked, ladle out 100 ml (3½ fl oz or scant ½ cup) of liquid from the casserole and whisk into the yolks. Pour back into the casserole and stir until the sauce has thickened; do not allow it to boil or it will curdle. Stir in the mint and serve sprinkled with the breadcrumb topping.

preparation time:
20 minutes, plus infusing
cooking time: about 20 minutes

serves 4

saffron threads
1 pinch

butter
50 g (2 oz or 4 tablespoons)

shallots
2, or 1 small onion, finely chopped

garlic
1 clove, crushed

rindless pancetta or streaky bacon
75 g (3 oz), cut into strips

fresh or frozen peas
500 g (1 lb), defrosted if frozen

gem lettuce
2 small, cut into wide strips

caster sugar
1–2 teaspoons

egg yolks
2, beaten

fresh mint
2 tablespoons chopped

salt and pepper

topping:

butter
25 g (1 oz or 2 tablespoons)

fresh white breadcrumbs
75 g (3 oz)

Parmesan or pecorino cheese
25 g (1 oz), finely grated

Lutein, found in peas, lettuce and other green vegetables, can help prevent the hardening of the arteries which may lead to heart disease.

green pea
stew
with saffron & mint

fresh or frozen small broad beans
250 g (8 oz), defrosted if frozen

sugar snap peas
175 g (6 oz), trimmed

young asparagus
175 g (6 oz), trimmed and cut into 2.5 cm (1 inch) pieces

butter
75 g (3 oz or 6 tablespoons)

spring onions
8, sliced

garlic
2 cloves, chopped

chicken or vegetable stock
900 ml (1½ pints or 3⅔ cups)

thyme
1 sprig

baby onions
15, peeled

baby turnips
10, or 3 small turnips, cut into wedges

baby carrots
250 g (8 oz)

lemon juice
1½ tablespoons

salt and pepper

fresh chervil, to garnish

serves 4

navarin
of spring vegetables

The chlorophyll in green **vegetables** offers many health benefits including helping combat anaemia and fatigue.

1 Blanch the broad beans, if using fresh, the sugar snap peas and asparagus separately in lightly salted boiling water and refresh immediately in cold water. Drain and set aside. Pop the broad beans out of their skins.

2 Melt the butter in a large flameproof casserole over a low heat, add the spring onions and garlic and cook, without colouring, until softened. Add the stock and thyme, bring to the boil and add the baby onions. Cover and simmer for 5 minutes.

3 Add the turnips, bring back to the boil, reduce the heat and simmer for 6–8 minutes. Add the carrots and cook for 5–6 minutes. Season with salt, pepper and lemon juice. Add the beans, sugar snap peas and asparagus and heat through. Serve garnished with the chervil.

preparation time:
20–25 minutes
cooking time: 25 minutes

tip:
You can vary the vegetables according to availability. Try adding artichoke hearts, new potatoes, baby leeks, fresh peas, patty pan squash or baby courgettes. Use fresh stock if possible.

stir-fried
arame seaweed
with tofu

Arame seaweed has a firm texture, which contrasts well with tofu. Packed with minerals and vitamins, **seaweed** provides healthy functioning of the thyroid and kidneys, and the immune, nervous and cardiovascular systems.

firm tofu
500 g (1 lb), thickly sliced

rice flour or plain flour, for dusting
25–50 g (1–2 oz or ¼–½ cup)

groundnut oil
10–12 tablespoons

arame seaweed
15 g (½ oz)

garlic
2 cloves, crushed

light soy sauce
3 tablespoons

mirin (rice wine)
6 tablespoons

clear honey
2 teaspoons

sesame oil
4 teaspoons

mangetouts
6, finely shredded

serves 4

1 Dust the tofu slices in rice flour or plain flour. Heat 8–10 tablespoons of the groundnut oil in a frying pan and fry the pieces of tofu, two at a time, for about 2–4 minutes, turning them once or until golden brown on all sides. Remove the tofu from the oil and drain on kitchen paper.

2 Soak the arame seaweed in boiling water for 30 minutes. Remove the seaweed and reserve the soaking water. Roughly chop any large strands of seaweed. Strain the soaking water and put 6 tablespoons of it in a saucepan with the garlic, soy sauce, mirin and honey and heat gently for 5 minutes.

3 Heat the remaining 2 tablespoons of groundnut oil in a wok or large frying pan. Return the tofu to the oil with the seaweed and stir-fry for 1 minute. Add the mirin and soy sauce to the hot pan and stir-fry quickly. Add the sesame oil and shredded mangetouts. Serve at once with boiled brown rice.

preparation time:
10 minutes, plus soaking
cooking time: 20 minutes

pak choi

750 g (1½ lb), trimmed

garlic

1 head, broken into cloves

water

150 ml (¼ pint or ⅔ cup)

groundnut or vegetable oil

3 tablespoons

tofu

125 g (4 oz), drained and cut into chunks

red chilli

1 large, deseeded and finely chopped

black bean sauce

2 tablespoons

oyster sauce

1 tablespoon

light soy sauce

2 tablespoons

serves 4

1 Cut any large pak choi in half or quarters and rinse well. Place the garlic cloves in a saucepan with the water. Bring to the boil. Stand the pak choi upright in the pan of boiling water and leave to cook for 5 minutes.

2 Remove the pak choi from the pan and drain. Remove the garlic from the boiling water and slip the cloves out of their skins. Reserve the boiling water.

3 Heat the oil in a wok, add the tofu and cook on all sides. Remove and reserve. Add the pak choi to the hot oil and toss in the oil for 2 minutes. Add the chopped chilli and the garlic cloves.

4 Working quickly, mix the black bean, oyster and soy sauces together with 6–8 tablespoons of the reserved vegetable water. Pour this mixture over the pak choi and toss together. Add the fried tofu and toss again carefully. Serve immediately with plain boiled rice.

preparation time: 20 minutes
cooking time: 15 minutes

Cabbage stimulates the immune system and is useful for killing off both bacteria and viruses.

braised pak choi with black bean & chilli sauce

1 First make the sauce. Heat the oil in a large saucepan and fry the onion and garlic until soft but not coloured. Stir in the curry paste, turmeric, sugar, coconut milk, lime juice, desiccated coconut and stock, mixing well to blend. Bring to the boil and cook quickly, stirring frequently, for 10–15 minutes to reduce the sauce slightly and concentrate the flavours.

2 Blend the cornflour with the cream to make a smooth paste. Add this to the sauce and cook for a few minutes to thicken, then stir in half of the fresh coriander. Add the mangetouts, courgettes and peas and simmer gently.

3 Steam the broccoli for 4 minutes, then add to the sauce and cook for a few minutes until all the vegetables are tender. Sprinkle with the remaining coriander and serve immediately with boiled rice.

preparation time: 15 minutes
cooking time: 25 minutes

serves 4

mangetouts
175 g (6 oz), trimmed and diagonally halved if large

courgettes
2 large, cut into 5 mm (¼ inch) slices

shelled peas
125 g (4 oz)

broccoli
250 g (8 oz), trimmed

coconut sauce:

vegetable oil
3 tablespoons

onion
1 large, finely chopped

garlic
4 cloves, finely chopped

green Thai curry paste
3–4 teaspoons

ground turmeric
2 teaspoons

brown sugar
2 teaspoons

coconut milk
2 x 400 g (13 oz) cans

lime
½, juice extracted

desiccated coconut
3 tablespoons

vegetable stock
175 ml (6 fl oz or ¾ cup)

cornflour
1 tablespoon

double cream
50 ml (2 fl oz or ¼ cup)

fresh coriander
4 tablespoons, chopped

salt and pepper

green vegetables
with
Thai coconut sauce

pak choi
500 g (1 lb)

broccoli
250 g (8 oz)

sunflower oil
3 tablespoons

light sesame oil
1 tablespoon

onion
1, quartered and thinly sliced

garlic
3 cloves, thinly sliced

water chestnuts
250 g (8 oz) can, drained and sliced

bean sprouts
50–75 g (2–3 oz or ¼–½ cup)

sesame seeds
2 tablespoons, toasted

black bean sauce:

cornflour
1 tablespoon

vegetable stock
300 ml (½ pint or 1¼ cups)

soy sauce
2–4 tablespoons

black bean sauce
2 tablespoons

sweet chilli sauce
2 teaspoons

clear honey
1 tablespoon

wilted greens
with water chestnuts
& black bean sauce

Green vegetables are superb sources of folic acid, carotenoids, vitamins C and K, calcium and iron.

1 First prepare the sauce. Put the cornflour in a bowl, gradually add about 2 tablespoons of the stock and mix to a smooth paste. Stir in the rest of the ingredients and season to taste. Set aside until required.

2 Shred the pak choi, but not too finely. Trim any woody stems from the broccoli and divide the head into florets each with a little stem.

3 Heat the sunflower and sesame oils in a large wok or frying pan, add the onion and garlic and stir-fry until soft but not coloured. Increase the heat, add the pak choi, broccoli and water chestnuts and stir-fry over a high heat for about 3–5 minutes until the vegetables are almost tender. Add the bean sprouts. Stir the black bean sauce then add to the pan, tossing the vegetables in it to coat thoroughly. Bring to the boil and cook for about 1 minute to thicken the sauce. Season to taste, sprinkle with the toasted sesame seeds and serve immediately with rice or noodles.

preparation time: 15 minutes
cooking time: 12 minutes

serves 4

stir-fried mixed vegetables with cashew nuts

Eat cruciferous vegetables like kale, cauliflower, broccoli and cabbage three times a week for the best of health.

Chinese leaves
250 g (8 oz), cut into 2.5 cm (1 inch) pieces

cauliflower florets
50 g (2 oz)

broccoli (preferably Chinese)
50 g (2 oz), divided into florets

white cabbage
50 g (2 oz), chopped

baby sweetcorn
2, diagonally sliced

tomato
1, cut into 8 pieces

garlic
5 cloves, chopped

cashew nuts
50 g (2 oz), toasted and crushed

soy sauce
1½ tablespoons

sugar
1 teaspoon

water
100 ml (3½ fl oz or scant ½ cup)

groundnut oil
2½ tablespoons

pepper

serves 4

1 Mix all the ingredients, except the oil, in a bowl.

2 Heat a wok and add the oil. Throw in the contents of the bowl and cook over a high heat, stirring and turning, for 2–3 minutes. Season with black pepper to taste. Serve at once.

preparation time: 20 minutes
cooking time: 2–3 minutes

chickpeas

2 x 400 g (13 oz) cans, drained and rinsed

vegetable stock

125–150 ml (4–5 fl oz or ½–⅔ cup)

fresh spinach

500 g (1 lb), washed

olive oil

2–3 tablespoons

onions

1–2 large, finely chopped

garlic

2–4 cloves, crushed

ground cumin

2 teaspoons

paprika

2 teaspoons

plum tomatoes

2 x 400 g (13 oz) cans

double concentrate tomato purée

1 tablespoon

fresh oregano

2 teaspoons finely chopped

mature Cheddar cheese

50 g (2 oz), grated

Parmesan cheese

25 g (1 oz), freshly grated

salt and pepper

serves 4–6

1 Blend half the chickpeas in a blender or food processor, adding enough stock to give a smooth paste.

2 Place the spinach leaves in a large saucepan with just the water that clings to the rinsed leaves. Cover and cook gently until tender, turning and shaking occasionally. This will take about 4 minutes.

3 Heat the oil in a large saucepan and fry the onions and garlic until soft but not coloured. Add the cumin and paprika along with the whole chickpeas and fry for a few minutes, stirring well. Add the spinach, tomatoes, tomato purée, chickpea purée and oregano. Season with salt and pepper. Bring to the boil, reduce the heat and simmer for 5–10 minutes until the flavours are blended and the stew rich and pulpy.

4 Stir in half of the Cheddar cheese until just melted, then divide among four to six 300–375 ml (10–13 fl oz or about ⅓ quart) gratin dishes. Mix the remaining Cheddar and Parmesan cheeses together and sprinkle over the stew. Place briefly under a preheated grill until the cheese is bubbling and forms a golden crust. Serve immediately with thick natural yogurt and a mixed leaf salad.

preparation time: 15 minutes
cooking time:
about 25 minutes

Spinach is believed to reduce the risk of some cancers, stroke and heart disease.

spinach
& chickpea
stew

chapter six

great
greens
for kids

1 Cook the macaroni in a saucepan of boiling water according to packet instructions until *al dente*. Meanwhile, steam the broccoli, carrot and peas in a steamer over another pan of boiling water for 6–7 minutes. Lift the steamer off the pan; keep covered.

2 Melt the butter in the dried steamer pan. Stir in the flour and cook for 1 minute, then gradually mix in the milk and bring to the boil, stirring until the sauce is thickened and smooth. Stir in the mustard, if using, and three-quarters of the cheese.

3 Drain the macaroni and stir into the sauce. Spoon two-thirds of the macaroni cheese into two 200 ml (7 fl oz or ⅕ quart) individual ovenproof dishes. Arrange the carrot, broccoli and peas in layers on top, then cover with the rest of the macaroni cheese.

4 Sprinkle with the remaining cheese and breadcrumbs and brown under a hot grill for 5 minutes. Set on serving plates and allow to cool slightly before serving, with cherry tomatoes.

preparation time: 15 minutes
cooking time:
about 15 minutes

tip:
Make this quick and easy pasta in heatproof glass dishes so that children can see and count the different layers.

dried macaroni
125 g (4 oz)

broccoli
100 g (3½ oz), divided into tiny florets, stems sliced

carrot
1, about 125 g (4 oz), sliced

frozen peas
50 g (2 oz)

butter
15 g (½ oz or 1 tablespoon)

plain flour
1 tablespoon

milk
200 ml (7 fl oz or scant 1 cup)

Dijon mustard (optional)
1 teaspoon

medium Cheddar cheese
100 g (3½ oz), grated

fresh breadcrumbs
1 tablespoon

quartered cherry tomatoes, to serve

serves 2

One portion of **broccoli** provides ten per cent of the recommended daily intake of calcium.

stripy macaroni cheese

pasta
with tomato,
spinach
& ricotta sauce

Its beneficial effect on energy, bone health and eyesight are three first-class reasons to give your kids spinach!

dried pasta shapes
375 g (12 oz)

olive oil
1 teaspoon

garlic
1 clove, crushed

onion
1, sliced

dried chilli flakes (optional)
½ teaspoon

passata
700 g (1 lb 6 oz) jar

fresh baby spinach
225 g (7½ oz), washed

ricotta cheese
150 g (5 oz)

salt and pepper

serves 4

1 Cook the pasta in a saucepan of lightly salted boiling water according to packet instructions and drain.

2 Meanwhile, heat the oil in a saucepan, add the garlic and onion and fry for 3–4 minutes. Add the chilli flakes, if using, and continue to fry for 1 minute.

3 Stir in the passata and simmer for 2 minutes. Add the spinach and ricotta, stir until the spinach has wilted then simmer for 3–4 minutes.

4 Toss the cooked pasta through the sauce, season to taste with salt and pepper and serve.

preparation time: 10 minutes
cooking time: 15 minutes

cheesy
spinach
lasagne

1 Put the fresh spinach in a large saucepan and cook gently with just the water that clings to the rinsed leaves; season with salt and pepper to taste. Drain thoroughly, then chop finely. Cook frozen spinach as instructed on the packet .

2 Heat the olive oil in a saucepan, add the onions and garlic and cook until tender. Mix with the cooked spinach and set aside.

3 To make the cheese sauce, heat the butter or margarine in a saucepan. Stir in the flour, then add the milk gradually. Bring to the boil, then stir or whisk into a smooth sauce.

4 Whisk the eggs, if using, into the hot, but not boiling sauce. Do not reheat. Stir most of the grated cheese into the sauce, with the prepared mustard and salt and pepper to taste.

5 Make layers of lasagne, spinach and sauce in an ovenproof dish, beginning with lasagne, and ending with lasagne topped by a coating of cheese sauce.

6 Sprinkle the remaining grated Gruyère or Cheddar and Parmesan over the top of the lasagne and bake in a preheated oven, 190°C/357°F/Gas 5, for 25–30 minutes. Serve hot.

preparation time: 25 minutes
cooking time: 40–45 minutes
oven temperature:
190°C/375°F/Gas 5

serves 4

fresh or frozen spinach
500–750 g (1–1½ lb) fresh, washed and chopped, or 375 g (12 oz) frozen

olive oil
1½ tablespoons

onions
2, finely chopped

garlic
2 cloves, finely chopped

ready-to-cook lasagne
10 sheets

salt and pepper

cheese sauce:

butter or margarine
50 g (2 oz or 4 tablespoons)

flour
50 g (2 oz or ½ cup)

milk
750 ml (1¼ pints or 3 cups)

eggs (optional)
1–2, beaten

Gruyère or Cheddar cheese
175 g (6 oz), grated

Parmesan cheese
2–3 tablespoons, freshly grated

prepared English mustard
1 teaspoon

green peppers
4 large

olive oil
1 tablespoon

onion
1, finely chopped

streaky bacon
50 g (2 oz), rinds removed and finely chopped

lean minced beef
175 g (6 oz)

breadcrumbs
4 tablespoons

egg
1, beaten

fresh parsley
1 tablespoon chopped

salt and pepper

sauce:

olive oil
2 tablespoons

tomatoes
250 g (8 oz) can

tomato purée
1 tablespoon

garlic
1 clove, crushed

brown sugar
1 teaspoon

wine vinegar
1 tablespoon

1 Cut the tops off the peppers and reserve. Scoop out the seeds with a spoon. Heat the oil in a saucepan and sauté the onion for 5 minutes. Stir in the bacon and beef and cook, turning, for 5 more minutes. Stir in the breadcrumbs. Remove the pan from the heat, stir in the egg and parsley and season with salt and pepper to taste. Stuff the peppers with this mixture, stand them upright in a deep ovenproof dish and replace the tops.

2 To prepare the sauce, gently heat the oil in a small pan, add the canned tomatoes and tomato purée and mix well. Add all of the remaining ingredients, season to taste and bring to the boil. Reduce the heat, cover and cook gently, stirring occasionally, for 10 minutes.

3 Pour the sauce over the peppers, cover and cook in a preheated oven, 160°C/325°F/Gas 3, for about 40 minutes. Serve hot.

preparation time: 15 minutes
cooking time: about 1 hour
oven temperature:
160°C/325°F/Gas 3

Serves 4

A **green pepper** provides twice as much vitamin C as a citrus fruit. Vitamin C helps boost the immune system and fight the effects of ageing, cancer and heart disease.

stuffed peppers

1 Melt 15 g (½ oz or 1 tablespoon) of the butter with the oil in a heavy-bottomed saucepan. Add the diced chicken and sauté gently for 2–3 minutes. Add the onion and sauté for 5 minutes, until softened but not coloured. Add the garlic and chilli and cook until the garlic is golden.

2 Add the rice to the pan and stir well to coat the grains with the butter and oil. Add the hot stock, a large ladleful at a time, stirring until each addition is absorbed into the rice. Continue adding stock in this way, cooking until the rice is creamy but the grains are still firm. This should take about 20 minutes.

3 Plunge the broccoli florets into a saucepan of boiling water for 1 minute. Drain thoroughly and add to the rice with the Parmesan. Season to taste with salt and pepper and stir in the remaining butter. Cover and leave the risotto to rest for a few minutes before serving.

preparation time: 10 minutes
cooking time: 30–35 minutes

butter
40 g (1½ oz or 3 tablespoons)

olive oil
2 tablespoons

boneless chicken breasts
2, skinned and diced

onion
½, very finely chopped

garlic
1 clove, finely chopped

fresh red chillies
1–2, deseeded and very finely chopped

risotto rice
300 g (10 oz)

hot chicken stock
1 litre (1¾ pints or 4 cups)

broccoli
250 g (8 oz), divided into florets

Parmesan cheese
3 tablespoons, freshly grated

salt and pepper

serves 4–6

As it is high in antioxidants, fibre and folic acid, **broccoli** is the easy way to good health.

spicy chicken
& broccoli
risotto

chicken & spinach potato pie

Spinach is a nutritious vegetable, rich in beta-carotene and vitamin C, and a useful source of folic acid, iron, potassium, calcium and magnesium.

sunflower or vegetable oil
2 tablespoons

onion
1, chopped

garlic
3 cloves, sliced

fresh root ginger
4 cm (1½ inches), finely shredded

boneless chicken thighs
6, skinned and cut into chunks

chicken stock
300 ml (½ pint or 1¼ cups)

creamed coconut (from a block)
75 g/3 oz

potatoes
875 g (1¾ lb), peeled and cut into pieces

semi-skimmed milk
5 tablespoons

fresh spinach
150 g (5 oz), washed and trimmed

freshly grated nutmeg, salt and pepper

serves 4

1 Heat the oil in a large frying pan or sauté pan. Add the onion, garlic, ginger and chicken pieces and fry gently for about 5 minutes until the chicken just begins to colour.

2 Add the stock and creamed coconut and bring to a simmer, stirring gently to blend the coconut into the liquid. Cover and cook gently for a further 10 minutes.

3 Meanwhile, cook the potatoes in a saucepan of lightly salted boiling water for about 15 minutes until soft. Drain, then return to the pan and mash with the milk.

4 Pile the spinach on top of the chicken mixture and cover with a lid. Leave to cook gently for 1–2 minutes until the spinach has wilted. Add plenty of nutmeg and a little salt and pepper, and stir the spinach into the sauce.

5 Turn into a 1.8 litre (3 pint or 2 quart) pie dish. Top with the mashed potato and rough up the surface with a fork. Bake the pie in a preheated oven at 180°C/350°F/Gas 4, for about 30 minutes until the surface is pale golden. Serve with a green vegetable, such as broccoli or peas.

preparation time: 20 minutes
cooking time: 50 minutes
oven temperature: 180°C/350°F/Gas 4

tip:

Creamed coconut – sold in blocks – has a more concentrated flavour than canned coconut milk, or coconut cream which is usually sold in cartons. Solid when cold, creamed coconut can become quite soft during hot weather. As well as adding an exotic flavour, creamed coconut acts as a natural thickener in sauce.

spinach
& ricotta
pancakes

Half a cup of cooked **spinach** contains more calcium, magnesium and iron than the same quantity of milk.

1 To make the pancakes, put the flour and salt in a bowl and make a well in the centre. Pour the egg and some of the milk into the well. Whisk the liquid, gradually incorporating the flour to make a smooth paste. Whisk in the remaining milk, then pour the batter into a measuring cup with a pouring spout. Allow to rest, if desired.

2 Heat a little oil or butter in an 18 cm (7 inch) crêpe pan or heavy-bottomed frying pan until it starts to smoke. Pour off the excess and pour a little batter into the pan, tilting it until the base is coated with a thin layer. Cook for 1–2 minutes until the underside begins to turn golden.

3 Flip the pancake with a spatula and cook for a further 30–45 seconds until it is golden on the second side. Slide the pancake out of the pan and keep warm. Make another seven pancakes in the same way, greasing the pan each time as necessary. Keep the them warm while you make the filling.

4 Stir the egg, ricotta and half of the Parmesan into the chopped, cooked spinach. Season with salt and pepper. Divide the mixture among the eight pancakes, then roll each up and place in a lightly greased, shallow baking dish. Dot with the butter, sprinkle with the remaining cheese and add the stock. Bake in a preheated oven at 200°/400°F/Gas 6 for 20 minutes. Serve immediately.

preparation time: 15 minutes, plus resting
cooking time: about 40 minutes

egg
1, beaten

ricotta cheese
250 g (8 oz)

Parmesan cheese
50 g (2 oz), freshly grated

cooked spinach
250 g (8 oz), chopped

butter
25 g (1 oz or 2 tablespoons)

chicken stock
150 ml (¼ pint or ⅔ cup)

salt and pepper

pancake batter:

plain flour
150 g (5 oz or 1¼ cups)

salt
1 pinch

egg
1, lightly beaten

milk
300 ml (½ pint or 1¼ cups)

light olive or vegetable oil or butter, for greasing

serves 4

broccoli
150 g (5 oz), divided into small florets

butter
40 g (1½ oz or 3 tablespoons)

Parmesan cheese
1 tablespoon, freshly grated

plain flour
25 g (1 oz or ¼ cup)

full-fat milk
150 ml (¼ pint or ⅔ cup)

double Gloucester cheese with chives, or medium Cheddar cheese
100 g (3½ oz), grated

Dijon mustard (optional)
1 teaspoon

cayenne pepper
1 pinch

eggs
3, separated

serves 4

1 Steam the broccoli for 3–4 minutes or until just tender. Meanwhile, grease four 200 ml (7 fl oz or ⅓ quart) individual soufflé dishes with a little of the butter, then sprinkle with the Parmesan.

2 Melt the remaining butter in a small saucepan, stir in the flour and cook for 1 minute. Gradually stir in the milk and bring to the boil, stirring until thick and smooth.

3 Take the pan off the heat and stir in the cheese, mustard, if using, and cayenne. Gradually beat in the egg yolks, one at a time.

4 Whisk the egg whites in a separate bowl until soft, moist peaks form. Stir a little of the egg white into the cheese mixture to lighten it, then carefully fold in the rest.

5 Divide the broccoli between the prepared dishes, then pour the cheese mixture over the top. Bake in a preheated oven at 190°C/375°F/Gas 5 for 15 minutes. Scoop the soufflés on to individual plates and serve with cherry tomatoes and warm toast.

preparation time: 15 minutes
cooking time: 20–25 minutes
oven temperature: 190°C/375°F/Gas 5

tip:
Pregnant women and young children should not eat softly cooked eggs, so make sure that the soufflé is well risen and cooked right through to the centre.

Regarded as the 'king of vegetables', broccoli is rich in vitamin C, beta-carotene and folic acid. Steaming rather than boiling broccoli helps preserve its water-soluble vitamin C content.

cheesy clouds

1 Put the onion in a large pan with the oil and fry until golden brown and softened. Add the milk, flour and herbs and slowly bring to the boil, whisking all the time.

2 Once the sauce is boiling, reduce the heat and cook for 2–3 minutes or until thickened. Add the tomatoes, salt and pepper and mix well.

3 Add the butter beans, broccoli and parsley to the sauce and bring to the boil, stirring. Pour into a lightly greased 1 litre (1¾ pint or 1 quart) ovenproof dish.

4 Mix the breadcrumbs with the grated cheese and sprinkle over the top. Cook in the centre of a preheated oven, 180°C/350°F/Gas 4, for 20–25 minutes or until the breadcrumbs are golden brown and the sauce is bubbling. Serve with a salad.

preparation time: 15 minutes
cooking time: 35 minutes
oven temperature:
180°C/350°F/Gas 4

onion
1 small, finely chopped

vegetable or olive oil
1 tablespoon

milk
300 ml (½ pint or 1¼ cups)

plain flour
2 tablespoons

dried mixed herbs
½ teaspoon

tomatoes
4, skinned, deseeded and chopped

organic butter beans
425 g (14 oz) can, drained

broccoli
150 g (5 oz), divided into small florets

fresh parsley
2 tablespoons chopped

wholemeal breadcrumbs
50 g (2 oz)

Parmesan or Cheddar cheese
1 tablespoon, freshly grated

salt and pepper

serves 4–6

With its free radical-fighting properties, broccoli helps protect cells in the brain and body from oxidative damage.

broccoli & butter bean bake

cabbage cups

with creamy carrot sauce

Although greens are the best of all, the more you vary the colours of the **vegetables** you eat, the greater the variety of beneficial plant chemicals you will get.

carrots or butternut squash
150 g (5 oz), thickly sliced

vegetable stock
400 ml (14 fl oz or 1¾ cups)

couscous
50 g (2 oz)

raisins
1 tablespoon

ready-to-eat dried apricots
2, chopped

red pepper
¼, deseeded and diced

frozen peas
2 tablespoons

ground allspice
1 pinch

olive oil
2 teaspoons

Savoy cabbage leaves
2, thick stems removed

salt and pepper

serves 2

1 Put the carrots or butternut and 300 ml (½ pint or 1¼ cups) of the stock in the base of a steamer pan and bring to the boil. Cover and simmer for 10 minutes. Meanwhile, put the couscous in a bowl, pour on the remaining hot stock and leave to soak for 5 minutes.

2 Add the raisins, apricots, red pepper, peas, allspice and oil to the soaked couscous and mix with a fork; season lightly with salt and pepper. Spoon the mixture on to the two cabbage leaves, folding up the sides of the leaves to encase the filling.

3 Place the cabbage cups into the steamer above the carrots. Cover and cook for 5 minutes until the cabbage is tender; keep the steamer covered.

4 Purée the carrots with half of the stock until smooth. Gradually blend in enough of the remaining stock to make a pouring sauce.

5 Spoon the sauce over the base of two serving dishes. Place the cabbage parcels on top and serve.

preparation time: 15 minutes
cooking time: 20 minutes

spinach,
onion & cream cheese
pizza

Immune-boosting and body-strengthening, **spinach** is one of the best green vegetables for all-round good health.

self-raising flour
250 g (8 oz or 2 cups)

olive oil
3 tablespoons

salt
1 teaspoon

water
7 tablespoons

topping:

full-fat soft cheese
100 g (3½ oz)

crème fraîche
100 ml (3½ fl oz or scant ½ cup)

fresh rosemary
2 teaspoons chopped

olive oil
3 tablespoons

onion
1 large, finely sliced

fresh baby spinach
375 g (12 oz), washed

salt and pepper

serves 4

1 To make the pizza base, place the flour in a bowl with the oil and salt. Add the water and mix to a soft dough, adding a little more water if the dough is too dry. Roll out on a floured surface into a round about 28 cm (11 inches) in diameter. Place on a large greased baking sheet and bake in a preheated oven, 230°C/450°F/Gas 8, for 5 minutes or until a crust has formed.

2 To make the topping, beat together the cream cheese, crème fraîche, rosemary and a little salt and pepper.

3 Heat the oil in a frying pan and sauté the onion for 3–4 minutes until softened. Add the spinach and a little salt and pepper and cook, stirring, for about 1 minute or until the spinach has just wilted.

4 Pile the spinach on to the pizza crust, spreading it to within 1 cm (½ inch) of the edge. Place spoonfuls of the cheese mixture over the spinach. Bake for 8 more minutes, or until the cheese turns golden.

preparation time: 15 minutes
cooking time: about 20 minutes
oven temperature: 230°C/450°F/Gas 8

self-raising flour
250 g (8 oz or 2 cups)

salt
1 teaspoon

warm water
150 ml (¼ pint or ⅔ cup)

topping:

olive oil
5 tablespoons

garlic
2 cloves, crushed

red onion
1, finely sliced

courgettes
2, thinly sliced lengthways

red pepper
1, cored, deseeded and cut into strips

yellow pepper
1, cored, deseeded and cut into strips

plum tomatoes
4, skinned, cored and cut into wedges

asparagus
500 g (1 lb), trimmed

thyme
4 sprigs, separated into leaves

basil leaves
1 handful, roughly torn

salt and pepper

1 To make the pizza base, place the flour and salt in a large bowl. Slowly add the water and mix to form a soft dough. When it has bound together, mix the dough with your hands into a ball. Turn the dough out on a lightly floured surface and knead until smooth and soft.

2 Divide the dough into four pieces and, with your hands and a rolling pin, flatten each as thinly as possible. The pizza rounds do not have to be exact circles: that is one of the charms of making your own pizzas! Make the pizzas just a bit smaller than your serving plates and as thin as you can.

3 Put the pizza bases on to warmed baking sheets, brush with a little of the olive oil, then arrange the vegetables on the bases, sprinkling them with the thyme leaves and roughly torn basil.

4 Season the pizzas generously with salt and pepper, drizzle with the remaining olive oil, and bake at the top of a preheated oven, 230°C/450°F/ Gas 8, for 10 minutes. The vegetables should be slightly charred around the edges as this adds to the flavour.

preparation time: 30 minutes
cooking time: 10 minutes
oven temperature:
230°C/450°F/Gas 8

serves 4

This vegetable pizza gets you well on the way to consuming your five daily portions of fruit and vegetables.

.fresh vegetable
pizza

chapter seven

greens on the side

1 Heat the olive oil in a large saucepan, add the onion, garlic, chilli and pancetta and sauté for 5 minutes or until soft.

2 To prepare the cavolo nero, trim any wilting leaves, then cut the heads in half lengthways. Remove and discard the hard central stem and coarsely chop the leaves.

3 Add the cavolo nero to the onion mixture and stir well. Pour in the chicken stock and season with salt and pepper. Cook for 4 minutes over a moderate heat, stirring all the time.

4 Finally, add the grated Parmesan and serve at once.

preparation time: 10 minutes
cooking time: 10 minutes

olive oil
1 tablespoon

onion
1, sliced

garlic
1 clove, crushed

red chilli
1, cored, deseeded and diced

pancetta
125 g (4 oz), diced

cavolo nero
1 head

chicken stock
75 ml (3 fl oz or generous ⅓ cup)

Parmesan cheese
75 g (3 oz), coarsely grated

salt and pepper

serves 4

Cavolo nero is an Italian kale with a strong taste. Since one-third of cancers (particularly bowel and stomach) are thought to be diet related, you can help protect yourself by eating your greens.

cavolo nero
with pancetta

quick spinach

Spinach may be considered a 'perfect food', thanks to its role in regulating blood pressure, supporting bone health and boosting the immune system.

pine nuts
75 g (3 oz)

olive oil
1 tablespoon

red onion
1, sliced

garlic
1 clove, crushed

tomatoes
4, skinned, cored and coarsely chopped

fresh spinach
1 kg (2 lb), washed and trimmed

butter
50 g (2 oz or 4 tablespoons)

nutmeg
1 pinch, freshly grated

salt and pepper

serves 4

1 Put the pine nuts in a heavy-bottomed frying pan and dry-fry until browned, stirring all the time as they cook very quickly. Set aside.

2 Heat the oil in a large saucepan, add the onion and garlic and sauté for 5 minutes.

3 Add the tomatoes, spinach, butter, nutmeg, and season with salt and pepper. Increase the heat to high and mix well. Cook for 3 minutes until the spinach has just started to wilt. Remove the pan from the heat, stir in the toasted pine nuts, and serve immediately.

preparation time: 10 minutes
cooking time: 10 minutes

tip:
If you need to wash the spinach, make sure that it is dry before you start to cook. Place it in a salad spinner or tea towel, and spin it around to disperse excess water.

steamed
broccoli
with mushrooms

Consume **broccoli** one to three times a week to benefit from its health-giving, internal cleansing, mood-enhancing and skin-improving properties.

1 Separate the broccoli florets and stalks. Peel the stalks and, if they are thick, cut them into thin slices lengthways.

2 Put the broccoli and mushrooms on a plate and sprinkle with the fish or soy sauce, salt and sugar.

3 Put the plate in a steamer and steam until cooked, about 7–10 minutes. Carefully remove the plate from the steamer.

4 To serve, mix a little soy sauce with a little sesame oil and sugar, heat it up in a small saucepan, then drizzle it over the steamed vegetables.

preparation time: 5 minutes, plus soaking
cooking time: 7–10 minutes

broccoli
200 g (7 oz)

dried shiitake mushrooms
10, soaked for 15–20 minutes, drained and cut into thirds

fish sauce or soy sauce
2 tablespoons

salt
½ teaspoon

sugar
½ teaspoon

soy sauce, sesame oil and sugar to serve

serves 4

olive oil
2 tablespoons

red onion
1, chopped

garlic
2 cloves, crushed

**pancetta or
unsmoked bacon**
125 g (4 oz), diced

puy lentils
175 g (6 oz)

**fresh or frozen
broad beans**
1 kg (2 lb)

marjoram
1 handful, chopped

**cooked fresh, or
canned artichoke
hearts**
8

butter
50 g (2 oz or 4 tablespoons)

flat leaf parsley
1 handful, chopped

salt and pepper

serves 4

1 Heat the oil in a heavy-bottomed saucepan, add the onion, garlic and pancetta and sauté for 5 minutes.

2 Add the lentils, broad beans and marjoram, season with salt and pepper, and cover with hot water. Mix well and simmer for 15 minutes. The water may need to be topped up during cooking if the mixture is getting too thick and sticking to the bottom of the pan. Keep stirring, just to be sure that it does not stick.

3 Add the artichoke hearts and cook for 5 minutes. The mixture should be thick and rich. Finally, stir in the butter and parsley, taste for seasoning, and serve immediately.

preparation time: 10 minutes
cooking time: 25 minutes

High in protein and fibre, broad beans are also a good source of calcium, iron, potassium and phosphorus, all minerals vital for health.

braised
broad beans
and lentils

1 Place the pine nuts under a preheated grill or in a heavy-bottomed frying pan and dry-fry until golden all over. Set aside.

2 Steam the broccoli or plunge it into boiling water for 2 minutes, then drain well and transfer to a bowl.

3 Melt the butter in a small saucepan, add the lemon juice and anchovies, and heat until the butter foams. Pour the melted butter over the broccoli, sprinkle with salt and pepper, and toss. To serve, top the broccoli with the Parmesan and toasted pine nuts.

preparation time: 10 minutes
cooking time: 10 minutes

pine nuts
75 g (3 oz)

broccoli
1 kg (2 lb), divided into florets

butter
50 g (2 oz or 4 tablespoons)

lemon juice
4 tablespoons

anchovy fillets
4, finely chopped

Parmesan cheese
75 g (3 oz), freshly grated

salt and pepper

serves 4

Broccoli plays a major role in fighting bowel cancer thanks to its sulforaphane, which helps deactivate cancer-causing substances in the gut.

broccoli
with
anchovies

wilted
spinach
& pine nuts
with raisins

A marvellous choice, spinach is one of the top 10 health-giving vegetables.

plump raisins
65 g (2½ oz or ½ cup)

olive oil
3 tablespoons

pine nuts
50 g (2 oz)

garlic
2 cloves, crushed

fresh baby spinach
625 g (1¼ lb), washed

lemon rind
1, finely grated

salt and pepper

serves 4

1 Place the raisins in a small bowl, cover with boiling water and leave for 5 minutes.

2 Meanwhile, heat the oil in a large frying pan or sauté pan and sauté the pine nuts until pale golden. Stir in the garlic.

3 Thoroughly drain the raisins and add to the pan with the spinach. Cook for about 1 minute, turning the ingredients together until the spinach has just wilted. Add the grated lemon rind, season to taste with salt and pepper, and serve immediately.

preparation time: 5 minutes, plus soaking
cooking time: 5 minutes

greens
with lemon oil

Crammed with antioxidants, carotenoids, B vitamins including folic acid, and minerals like iron and calcium, green vegetables are infinitely more nutritious than non-green vegetables.

mixed salad greens (e.g. spinach, rocket, chard)
1 kg (2 lb)

olive oil
4 tablespoons

garlic
1 clove, crushed

lemon
½ small, juice extracted

salt and pepper

serves 4

1 Wash all the salad greens well, discarding the thick stalks from the spinach and chard, if using. Transfer the greens with just the water that clings to the rinsed leaves to a large saucepan. Heat gently, stirring until the leaves are wilted.

2 Strain off as much excess liquid as possible, then return the leaves to the pan and stir in the oil, garlic, lemon juice and salt and pepper to taste. Heat gently for 2–3 minutes, until the greens are tender. Serve immediately, to accompany fish, chicken or pork.

preparation time: 10 minutes
cooking time: 5 minutes

broccoli

375 g (12 oz), divided into small florets

cauliflower

250 g (8 oz), divided into small florets

pine nuts

2 tablespoons, toasted and chopped

thinly sliced red pepper, to garnish

dressing:

tarragon vinegar

2 tablespoons

coarse grain mustard

2 tablespoons

olive oil

1 tablespoon

fromage frais or natural yogurt

2 tablespoons

salt and pepper

serves 4

1 Cook the broccoli and cauliflower florets in a saucepan of lightly salted boiling water for 5 minutes. Drain thoroughly, put in a bowl, and cover to keep warm.

2 Make the dressing by mixing together the vinegar, mustard, salt and pepper, then gradually whisk in the oil until it thickens. Stir in the fromage frais or yogurt and pour the dressing over the florets, tossing carefully until they are well coated.

3 Arrange in a serving dish and sprinkle with the pine nuts. Serve garnished with red pepper strips.

preparation time: 10–15 minutes
cooking time: 5 minutes

Broccoli, also known as 'poor man's asparagus', is packed with a cocktail of vitamins and minerals.

warm
broccoli
vinaigrette

1 Heat the oil in a large frying pan. When hot, add the cumin and coriander seeds and the onion. Stir-fry until the onion is soft and light brown, then add the spinach and tomatoes and stir well.

2 Add the chilli powder, dhana jeera, amchur, jaggery or sugar and lime juice and stir. Cook for 1–2 minutes, then add the chickpeas and water.

Season with salt and pepper, cover and simmer gently for 10 minutes, stirring occasionally. Serve hot.

preparation time: 5 minutes
cooking time: 20 minutes

serves 4

vegetable oil
1 tablespoon

cumin seeds
1 teaspoon

coriander seeds
½ teaspoon coarsely ground

onion
1 small, finely chopped

fresh baby spinach
250 g (8 oz), washed

chopped tomatoes
200 g (7 oz) can

chilli powder
1 teaspoon

dhana jeera (spice mixture containing ground coriander and ground cumin)
1 tablespoon

amchur (dried mango powder)
1 teaspoon

jaggery or soft brown sugar
1 teaspoon

fresh lime juice
1 tablespoon

chickpeas
400 g (13 oz) can, drained and rinsed

water
175 ml (6 fl oz or ¾ cup)

salt and pepper

Since it is rich in calcium and magnesium, eating **spinach** regularly may protect against osteoporosis.

spinach
& chickpea
sabzi

provençal
peppers

Rich in vitamin C, green peppers have antibacterial properties and help normalize blood pressure.

oil
1 tablespoon

onions
2, sliced

green peppers
4, cored, deseeded and sliced

garlic
1 clove, crushed

chopped tomatoes
400 g (13 oz) can

fresh chopped herbs
2 teaspoons, or 1 teaspoon dried mixed herbs

salt and pepper

serves 4

1 Heat the oil in a pan, add the onions and fry until soft. Add the peppers and garlic and cook for 5 minutes.

2 Stir in the canned tomatoes and their juice, herbs and salt and pepper to taste. Bring to the boil, then simmer, uncovered, for 15 minutes. Transfer to a serving dish and serve hot or cold.

preparation time: 5 minutes
cooking time: 25–30 minutes

stir-fried leaf vegetables

Dark green leafy vegetables, like spinach, cabbage and lettuce, provide calcium, which helps strengthen bones.

1 Heat the oil in a wok, toss in the leafy green vegetables and stir-fry for 30 seconds. Add the oyster sauce, sugar and stock and cook for about 3 minutes, stirring all the time, until the leaves have wilted.

2 Turn on to a serving dish and sprinkle the garlic oil on the top.

preparation time: 5 minutes
cooking time: 5 minutes

oil
2 tablespoons

mixed leafy green vegetables (e.g. spinach, Chinese cabbage, lettuce, watercress)
325 g (11 oz), torn

oyster sauce
2 tablespoons

palm sugar or light muscovado sugar
1 teaspoon

vegetable stock
2 tablespoons

garlic oil
2 teaspoons

serves 4

pine nuts

4 tablespoons

vegetable oil

2 tablespoons

broccoli

175 g (6 oz), divided into small florets, stalks chopped

cauliflower

175 g (6 oz), divided into florets, stalks chopped

garlic

3 cloves, crushed

pepper

sauce:

cornflour

2 teaspoons

cold vegetable stock

6 tablespoons

soy sauce

2 tablespoons

lemon juice

1 tablespoon

serves 4

1 Heat a wok until hot. Add the pine nuts and dry-fry over a gentle heat for 1–2 minutes or until toasted. Remove the wok from the heat and tip out the pine nuts. Set aside.

2 Prepare the sauce ingredients. Mix the cornflour to a paste with 2 tablespoons of the stock, then add the remaining stock, the soy sauce and lemon juice. Set aside.

3 Return the wok to a moderate heat, add the oil and heat until hot. Add the broccoli and cauliflower stalks, increase the heat to high and stir-fry for 1 minute. Add the florets and garlic and stir-fry for a further 2–3 minutes or until the vegetables are tender but still crunchy.

4 Stir the sauce to mix, pour into the wok and bring to the boil, stirring constantly. Add pepper to taste and serve at once, sprinkled with the toasted pine nuts.

preparation time: 10 minutes
cooking time: about 10 minutes

Eat more cruciferous vegetables (like broccoli and cauliflower) to lower your chances of developing bowel cancer.

broccoli
& cauliflower
with pine nuts

1 Place the Brussels sprouts in a saucepan of lightly salted boiling water. Cover and cook for 10–12 minutes until tender.

2 Meanwhile, put the chestnuts in a saucepan, add enough vegetable stock to cover, and heat gently until warmed through.

3 Drain the sprouts and the chestnuts. Stir the chestnuts into the sprouts with the butter and season.

preparation time: 10 minutes
cooking time: 10–12 minutes

Brussels sprouts
750 g (1½ lb), trimmed

chestnuts
200 g (7 oz) can, drained

vegetable stock,
to cover

butter
15 g (½ oz or 1 tablespoon)

salt and pepper

serves 5

Brussels sprouts are believed to be a very potent preventer of cancer, particularly breast and bowel cancer.

Brussels sprouts
with chestnuts

colcannon

Cabbage has deep cleansing and purifying properties: the water in which **cabbage** has been boiled is an age-old pick-me-up for a tired complexion.

kale or green leaf cabbage
500 g (1 lb), stalk removed, finely shredded

potatoes
500 g (1 lb), unpeeled

spring onions or chives
6, finely chopped

milk or cream
150 ml (¼ pint or ⅔ cup)

butter
125 g (4 oz or 1 stick)

salt and pepper

serves 4–6

1 Heat a saucepan of lightly salted water and boil the kale or cabbage in boiling water until very tender – about 10 minutes. At the same time heat another saucepan of lightly salted water and boil the potatoes until tender. Place the spring onions or chives and the milk or cream in a pan and simmer over a low heat for about 5 minutes.

2 Drain the kale or cabbage and mash. Drain the potatoes, peel and mash well. Add the hot milk mixture, beating well to give a soft fluffy texture. Beat in the kale or cabbage, season with salt and pepper and add half the butter. The colcannon should be a speckled, green colour. Heat through thoroughly before serving in individual bowls. Make a well in the centre of each and put a knob of the remaining butter in each one. Serve immediately.

preparation time: 20 minutes
cooking time: 20 minutes

seaweed & cucumber salad

with rice wine & vinegar dressing

Seaweed is packed with iodine, iron, calcium, zinc, magnesium and potassium, and its inclusion in the diet is believed to reduce the risk of cancer.

1 Place the seaweed in a bowl, cover with cold water and leave to stand for 15–20 minutes to soften.

2 Cut the cucumber in half lengthways, then slice it very thinly into half moons. Drain the seaweed and roughly chop any large pieces. Put the chopped seaweed in a bowl with the sliced cucumber.

3 Mix the mirin with the rice wine vinegar and sugar and heat very gently in a small saucepan until the sugar has dissolved. Remove from the heat and allow to cool, then add the lemon juice.

4 Pour the dressing over the seaweed and cucumber and toss lightly. Serve as an accompaniment to grilled fish.

preparation time: 10 minutes, plus soaking
cooking time: 3–4 minutes

tip:
This salad is best made with the mixed bags of seaweed and sea lettuces available in Chinese and oriental stores.

mixed dried seaweed (e.g. dulse, sea lettuce)
25 g (1 oz)

cucumber
1 small

mirin (rice wine)
75 ml (3 fl oz or generous ⅓ cup)

rice wine vinegar
75 ml (3 fl oz or generous ⅓ cup)

golden caster sugar
2 tablespoons

lemon juice
2 tablespoons

serves 4

vegetable oil
2 tablespoons

cumin seeds
1 teaspoon

onion
1, halved and finely sliced

fresh red chilli
1, finely sliced

garlic
3 cloves, finely chopped

broccoli
300 g (10 oz), divided into small florets

salt and pepper

serves 4

1 Heat the oil in a large, nonstick frying pan and, when hot, add the cumin seeds. Stir-fry for 1 minute then add the onion. Cook over a moderate heat until lightly browned.

2 Stir in the chilli, garlic and broccoli. Cover the pan and reduce the heat to low. Cook for 6–8 minutes, until the broccoli is just tender. Season with salt and pepper and serve hot to accompany a heavily spiced curry.

preparation time: 10 minutes
cooking time: 15 minutes

Dark green vegetables are strongly associated with cancer protection, particularly those like broccoli with high concentrations of sulforaphane, a cancer-fighting compound.

broccoli sabzi

chapter eight

supergreen

juices

kale & hearty

Kale is packed with calcium. Wheatgrass is high in chlorophyll, which combats anaemia, while spirulina, a form of chlorophyll from the blue-green algae family, is one of the best sources of vitamin B12, which is essential for the functioning of all cells.

1 Juice the kale and wheatgrass, then stir in the spirulina powder. Serve in a small glass decorated with wheatgrass blades.

preparation time: 3 minutes

kale
25 g (1 oz), washed

wheatgrass
100 g (3½ oz)

spirulina
1 teaspoon

makes 50 ml
(2 fl oz or ¼ cup)

famous five

This juice includes the top five vegetables that produce natural insulin. Brussels sprouts contain ingredients important for detoxifying the body and also have high antioxidant properties. Green beans supply antioxidants and folic acid. Lettuce is rich in vitamin K which promotes blood clotting.

1 Wash all the vegetables and juice them with the lemon. Serve decorated with slivers of green bean and carrot, if liked.

preparation time: 5 minutes

Brussels sprouts
100 g (3½ oz)

carrot
100 g (3½ oz)

Jerusalem artichokes
100 g (3½ oz)

green beans
100 g (3½ oz)

lettuce
100 g (3½ oz)

lemon
½

makes 200 ml (7 fl oz or scant 1 cup)

iron maiden

fresh spinach
250 g (8 oz), washed

carrot
250 g (8 oz), scrubbed

fresh parsley
25 g (1 oz)

spirulina
1 teaspoon

makes 200 ml (7 fl oz or scant 1 cup)

Juiced **spinach** makes a powerful cleansing drink. The folic acid in **spinach** builds up red blood cells, while its chlorophyll helps to combat fatigue. Spirulina provides a valuable boost of vitamin B12.

1 Juice the spinach, carrot and parsley and stir in the spirulina. Serve in a tumbler, decorated with carrot slivers if liked.

preparation time: 5 minutes

well healed

carrot
250 g (8 oz), scrubbed

green cabbage
250 g (8 oz)

Raw carrot and **cabbage** juices are notable for having a healing effect on stomach ulcers.

1 Juice the vegetables and serve in a tall glass over ice.

preparation time: 3 minutes

sticks & stones

Turnip-top leaves contain more calcium than milk. Broccoli also contains calcium and folic acid. Dandelion leaves are an excellent source of magnesium, which helps the body to utilize the calcium for healthy bones and teeth.

1 Scrub the turnip and carrot. Juice all the ingredients and whiz in a blender with a couple of ice cubes. Serve in a tall glass decorated with dandelion leaves, if liked.

preparation time: 5 minutes

turnips, including the tops
125 g (4 oz)

carrot
125 g (4 oz)

broccoli
125 g (4 oz)

dandelion leaves
1 handful

apple
175 g (6 oz)

makes 200 ml (7 fl oz or scant 1 cup)

twister

The salicylic acid in grapefruit works to break down uric acid deposits, while the carrot and spinach help to rebuild and regenerate cartilage and joints.

1 Peel the grapefruit, keeping as much of the pith as possible. Juice all the ingredients and serve in a tumbler. Decorate with slices of grapefruit, if liked.

preparation time: 5 minutes

pink grapefruit
125 g (4 oz)

carrot
125 g (4 oz), scrubbed

fresh spinach
125 g (4 oz), washed

makes 200 ml (7 fl oz or scant 1 cup)

what's up broc?

broccoli
250 g (8 oz)

carrot
175 g (7 oz), scrubbed

beetroot, scrubbed
50 g (2 oz)

makes 200 ml (7 fl oz
or scant 1 cup)

High in selenium, this is an ideal juice for smokers, to help guard against lung cancer.

1 Juice all the ingredients and serve in a tall glass. Decorate with a sprig of coriander, if liked.

preparation time: 5 minutes

spring clean

pear
250 g (8 oz)

cabbage
125 g (4 oz)

celery
50 g (2 oz)

watercress
25 g (1 oz)

makes 200 ml (7 fl oz
or scant 1 cup)

This juice is ideal for detoxing your system. The cabbage and pear rid the colon of waste matter and celery purifies the lymph. The watercress is high in calcium and iron.

1 Juice all the ingredients and serve over ice, decorated with celery sticks, if liked.

preparation time: 5 minutes

squeaky green

In this detoxing juice carrots, lettuce and celery all work to regenerate the liver and lymph systems and aid digestion. Both spinach and lettuce are rich in vitamin K which promotes blood clotting, while parsley is good for kidney stones.

1 Juice the ingredients and whiz in a blender with a couple of ice cubes. Decorate with parsley sprigs, if liked.

preparation time: 5 minutes

carrot
175 g (6 oz), scrubbed

fresh spinach
100 g (3½ oz), washed

lettuce
100 g (3½ oz)

celery
75 g (3 oz)

fresh parsley
25 g (1 oz)

makes 200 ml (7 fl oz or scant 1 cup)

green peace

The ingredients in this ultra green juice help to maintain energy levels.

1 Juice all the ingredients and serve in a glass over ice. Decorate with kale, if liked.

preparation time: 5 minutes

broccoli
100 g (3½ oz)

kale
100 g (3½ oz)

fresh parsley
25 g (1 oz)

apple
200 g (7 oz)

celery
50 g (2 oz)

makes 200 ml (7 fl oz or scant 1 cup)

way to go

pear
250 g (8 oz)

pitted prunes
25 g (1 oz)

fresh spinach
125 g (4 oz), washed

makes 200 ml (7 fl oz
or scant 1 cup)

This juice is good for constipation, containing a dose of three potent laxatives that will get you back on line.

1 Juice all the ingredients and serve in a tall glass over ice cubes. Decorate with pear slices, if liked.

preparation time: 5 minutes

energy burst

fresh spinach
125 g (4 oz), washed

apple
250 g (8 oz)

yellow pepper
100 g (3½ oz)

cinnamon
1 pinch

makes 200 ml (7 fl oz
or scant 1 cup)

Thanks to its slow release of energy when eaten, spinach is an energizing food and effective for combating long-term fatigue.

1 Juice all the ingredients and serve in a glass. If liked, add a cinnamon stick for decoration.

preparation time: 5 minutes

index